European Distance and E-Learning Network Annual Conference (EDEN 2019)

Connecting through Educational Technology to Produce Effective Learning Environments

Book of Abstracts

Bruges, Belgium
16 – 19 June 2019

Editors:

Airina Volungeviciene
Andras Szucs

ISBN: 978-1-7138-2383-4

Printed from e-media with permission by:

Curran Associates, Inc.
57 Morehouse Lane
Red Hook, NY 12571

Some format issues inherent in the e-media version may also appear in this print version.

For permission requests, please contact the publisher:

European Distance and E-Learning Network (EDEN)
Budapest University of Technology & Economics
H-1111 Budapest, Egry J. u.1.
Hungary

secretariat@eden-online.org

Additional copies of this publication are available from:

Curran Associates, Inc.
57 Morehouse Lane
Red Hook, NY 12571 USA
Phone: 845-758-0400
Fax: 845-758-2633
Email: curran@proceedings.com
Web: www.proceedings.com

EDEN 2019 ANNUAL Conference

Connecting through Educational Technology

to produce effective learning environments

EDEN 2019 Annual Conference

Bruges, Belgium

16-19 June 2019

BOOK OF ABSTRACTS

Including the Collection of "Synergy" Synopses

Edited by

Airina Volungeviciene, András Szűcs
on behalf of the European Distance and E-Learning Network

European Distance and E-Learning Network, 2019

EDEN 2019 Annual Conference
Bruges, Belgium

Published by the European Distance and E-Learning Network

Editors:

Airina Volungeviciene
András Szűcs

Editorial co-ordination:

Judit Kőműves
Gábor Román

EDEN Secretariat, c/o Budapest University of Technology and Economics
H-1111 Budapest, Egry J. u. 1, Hungary
Tel: (36) 1 463 1628, 463 2537
E-mail: secretariat@eden-online.org
http://www.eden-online.org

Conference organised in collaboration with

vives University of Applied Sciences KU Leuven Association

Principal Sponsor

televic education

Conference Publication Sponsor

Standaard Boekhandel
Je vindt er meer dan je zoekt

Conference Sponsors

foursevens
Signpost
Blackboard
Simulise

Supported by the Erasmus+ Programme of the European Union
The publication reflects the authors' view, the EACEA and the European Commission are not responsible for any use that may be made of the information it contains.

Introduction

Connecting through Educational Technology – to produce Effective Learning Environments

Technology is with us everywhere which validates the horizontal-holistic approach for imperative questions of the period. For the transforming education landscape, challenges come increasingly from the socio-cultural-economic, structural and policy fields. Education has to be visionary to reach efficiency gains, new sources – and to offer sustainable services, reflecting the complexity of modern societies.

Market realities put similar pressures on the corporate and University worlds. Stakeholders expect academia to respond to needs beyond teaching and research, better promote innovation and the knowledge economy, manage the new student populations. Universities are expected to detect and attract talents, be magnet of inputs from practitioners, resulting cooperative surplus.

Vocationalisation of education also means the emergence of new skill sets. The progress in industrial automation and ICTs opens possibilities for lifelong learning resources, for work based learning and integration of human-machine intelligence models.

Educational technologies are about connections among information, knowledge, action, emotion and value: knowledge construction, learning activities by sharing and thinking, interactivity, aggregative mechanisms, cooperation and integration – to meet the requirements of the knowledge age, to satisfy the needs of social transformation and learning innovation.

New generation of learning technologies and networks are ubiquitous, embedded and mobile which reshape access to and delivery of learning. Cutting edge fields are artificial intelligence, learning analytics, micro-learning, new credentialing, revolution of assessment, massive open online courses (MOOCs), personalized learning, game-based learning, flipped classroom, Digital Makerspaces and alike.

> *The questions remain: Which one(s) of these will have significant and sustained impact in the future? Can the network society become an enhanced learning society? How can information and communication technology in the age of Industry 4.0 create and enhance synergies between online learning programmes, the increased diversity of stakeholders, the workplace experience, socio-cultural influences and students' work-life balance?*

EDEN is pleased to welcome again at its 2019 Annual Conference the scholars, practitioners, experts from Europe and all around the world in Bruges to discuss the issues of Connecting through Educational Technology.

Major themes of the Conference included:

- *Global connections*: How to organise online study programmes that enhance the students' competences, provide connections with international partners and promote virtual mobility?
- *Connections with workplace*: How can innovative study programmes be developed to involve the workplace impact and experience (virtual dual learning, (distance/digital) internships)?
- *Connections with the community*: How to organise study programmes that focus on relations of curriculum, delivery and the socio-economic environment?
- *Connection with learners*: Caring about the work-life balance of the students, attentive to learners' needs, expectations and the changing behaviour of diverse student populations.

Andras Szucs	Sylke Vandercruysse	Airina Volungeviciene
Secretary General	VIVES University of Applied Sciences	President, EDEN

Acknowledgement and thanks are given to the Programme and Evaluation Committee

Airina Volungeviciene, EDEN President, Vytautas Magnus University, Lithuania
Isabel Vanslembrouck, Director of the Research Unit, VIVES University of Applied Sciences, Belgium

Diana Andone, Politehnica University of Timisoara, Romania

Ulrich Bernath, Ulrich Bernath Foundation for Research in ODL, Germany

Lisa Marie Blaschke, Carl von Ossietzky University of Oldenburg, Germany

Mark Brown, National Institute for Digital Learning, Dublin City University, Ireland

Elena Caldirola, University of Pavia, Italy

Helga Dorner, Central European University, Hungary

Josep Maria Duart, Universitat Oberta de Catalunya (UOC), Spain

Ulf-Daniel Ehlers, Co-Operative State University Baden-Wurttemberg (DHBW), Germany

Kurt Galle, VIVES University of Applied Sciences, Belgium

Rebecca Galley, The Open University, United Kingdom

Sandra Kucina Softic, University of Zagreb, Croatia

Mark Nichols, The Open University, United Kingdom

Don Olcott Jr., Carl von Ossietzky University of Oldenburg, Germany

Ebba Ossiannilsson, Swedish Association of Distance Education, Sweden

Wim Van Petegem, Katholieke Universiteit Leuven, Belgium

Antonella Poce, University Roma III, Italy

Timothy Read, National University of Distance Education (UNED), Spain

Alfredo Soeiro, University of Porto, Portugal

Andras Szucs, Secretary General, EDEN, United Kingdom

Ferenc Tatrai, EDEN, United Kingdom

Leen Thys, VIVES University of Applied Sciences, Belgium

Sylke Vandercruysse, VIVES University of Applied Sciences, Belgium

Delphine Wante, VIVES University of Applied Sciences, Belgium

TABLE OF CONTENTS

INSTITUTIONAL INNOVATION: STRATEGY AND PRACTICE

LEARNING AND TRAINING FOR WORK: CONCEPT AND IMPLEMENTATION

DIGITAL LEARNING THEORY AND GOVERNANCE

SOCIO-CULTURAL FEATURES OF ICT ENHANCED LEARNING

COLLABORATIVE LEARNING IN ONLINE ENVIRONMENTS

QUALITY, ASSESSMENT AND EVALUATION

LEARNER PERCEPTIONS, CHARACTERISTICS AND ATTITUDES

POLICY DEVELOPMENT IN ORGANIZATIONS

MOOCS: ENRICHING AND CONSOLIDATING THE EXPERIENCE

SELECTED LEADING RESEARCH AND INNOVATION CASES

INTERNATIONAL AND NATIONAL LEARNING DEVELOPMENT CASES

OPEN EDUCATION RESOURCES – STRATEGY AND PRACTICE

TEACHERS PROFESSIONAL EDUCATION AND ICTS

APPLICATIONS OF GAMES AND NEW ICT TOOLS IN EDUCATION

POSTERS

WORKSHOPS

DEMONSTRATIONS

SYNERGIES

IMPLEMENTATION OF A FLEXIBLE LEARNING STUDY PROGRAMME IN A BLENDED-LEARNING DESIGN: RESULTS OF THE FIRST TWO COHORTS

Claude Müller, Reinhild Fengler, Zurich University of Applied Sciences, Switzerland

Our society is subject to a constant process of transformation, and flexibility plays an increasingly important role in various areas of life. Accordingly, more flexibility is expected from universities as well, and in recent years, flexible learning has come into the focus of pedagogical quality development. The current discussion on the digitalization of education is also strongly influenced by the concept of flexible learning, hence, flexible learning, digital learning, blended or distance learning are often used synonymously.

Zurich University of Applied Sciences (ZHAW) launched the flexible study format FLEX, a blended learning design allowing students increased flexibility as to when and where they study. The Bachelor in Business Administration with a Specialization in Banking and Finance (BSc BA BF) was selected as the first to be offered in the FLEX study programme format. It is already being run in a full-time (FT) and in a part-time (PT) format. The FLEX format is the third study format for this degree programme. In the part-time programme, classroom lessons are held on two days a week during the term, while the FLEX format schedules classroom lessons for two days approximately every three weeks. Thus, FLEX reduces classroom learning time by about half, while adding an e-learning environment for self-study that includes instructional videos. For the assessment level (first three semesters), it was analysed how the students evaluate the learning environment and to what extent the results of the end-of-semester examinations of the experimental and control groups differ from one another.

The research design consists of the first two cohorts of the experimental group FLEX (cohort 15, $N = 28$; cohort 16, $N = 28$) with students attending all courses in the new FLEX format and the corresponding cohorts of the control group PT (cohort 15, $N = 100$; cohort 16, $N = 117$). All students are university freshmen, and the student eligibility requirements, lecture content, exam questions, and grading scale were identical for all students FLEX and PT in all courses.

Standardized student evaluations at course level are carried out at the end of each semester, in which indicators such as course structure, teaching or content quality are surveyed. The global indicator shows with an average of 3.18 (on a 4-level-scale, with 4.0 being the highest value) across all courses of FLEX, very similar values as for the conventional PT format (3.20). The survey also proved that the investment in setting up a video studio for the production of short learning videos was perceived as very positive: "Watching learning videos" is described by all students in all FLEX cohorts as the most beneficial activity for learning.

The exam results for Cohort 15 show that the mean values differ only slightly. In 8 of the 11 courses examined, the mean values of the FLEX cohort are higher than those of the PT students. The results of the t-test do not show any significant differences in the exam results between FLEX and PT students. To consider a possible bias at the entry competence level of the first FLEX cohort, the exam results of the second year (Cohort 16) were also analysed. Cohort 16 of the FLEX format also has higher mean values than the control group of PT students (in 8 out of 11 courses). Significant differences can be observed for three courses. FLEX students achieved significantly better exam results in these courses compared to the PT students. The FLEX results confirm previous findings regarding blended learning which have shown that students in blended learning courses produce at least equivalent or even slightly better exam results compared to students on face-to-face courses. However, a selection bias in the selection of the study format, i.e., that systematically high performing students opt for the FLEX programme, cannot be ruled out and must be examined more closely in subsequent research.

In summary, it can be concluded that the implementation of the FLEX programme has succeeded in creating an effective learning environment and a satisfactory learning organization for the students. This was certainly due to the relatively high investment that was made to meet the requirements of a successful change. A strategy and a vision were formulated, and the transformation was materially and technically supported, including substantial investment in the technical infrastructure.

VALIDATION OF THE COMMUNITY OF INQUIRY SURVEY (SPANISH VERSION) AT UNED COURSES

Inés Gil-Jaurena, Daniel Domínguez Figaredo, Belen Ballesteros Velázquez, Javier Morentin Encina, Universidad Nacional de Educación a Distancia (UNED), Spain

Between March and December 2018, within the frame of the CO-Lab Teaching Innovation Group at the Universidad Nacional de Educación a Distancia (UNED), we undertook a research and teaching innovation project, funded by the Vice-Rectorate for Methodology and Innovation. The project (ref. GID2016-30) was focused on the analysis, using the "Community of Inquiry" (CoI) theoretical model, of the educational practices developed in 25 Bachelor and Master distance courses in the Faculties of Education and Philosophy, with the aim of making proposals for improvement based on the analysis. We used the CoI survey (Arbaugh et al., 2008), originally developed in English. Its application in our case required a translation into Spanish and adaptation to the UNED context. Hence, one of our objectives was to undertake this task and validate the internal consistency of the CoI survey in the Spanish version.

The Community of Inquiry conceptual framework, widely used in online education, represents a process of creating a deep and meaningful (collaborative-constructivist) learning experience through the development of three interdependent elements: social, cognitive and teaching presence (The Community of Inquiry, 2017).

The CoI survey is a 34-items questionnaire which sought to reflect to what extent the three dimensions or interdependent presences (teacher, social and cognitive) were perceived by students in their learning experiences on digital platforms, based on constructivist and collaborative approaches of the CoI model. The survey uses a Likert-type scale. The validation of the CoI survey in different contexts of distance learning and different languages (English, Korean, Tuskish) offers, as a general result, the verification of the theoretical structure of the instrument, as well as a high reliability from the point of view of its internal consistency.

The Spanish version of the survey we have adapted consists of 34 questions with a Likert rating scale of 1 to 5 points. Thirteen questions correspond to the teaching presence, nine to the social presence and twelve to the cognitive presence (similarly to the original survey in English). We have published and distributed the Spanish version in a journal article (Ballesteros, Gil-Jaurena & Morentin, 2019).

We converted the survey into an online form using Google forms, and distributed it through 25 online courses (Undergraduate and Master level). We collected 162 students' replies, 75% of them female students (in accordance with the profile of the students in the Faculty of Education). The average age was 37 years old. The majority (76.5%) were studying a Bachelor programme.

The validation process shown the following:

- Construct validity was analysed through exploratory factor analysis. The results of the matrix of rotated factor structure indicates the adjustment of the dimensions to the theoretical structure.
- Reliability was analysed from the internal consistency approach, using the Cronbach alpha statistic. The results show values of 0.921, 0.926 and 0.938 in the teaching, social and cognitive dimensions, respectively, so we can justify that the CoI survey in its Spanish version has a high level of reliability and can be used as a measuring instrument in other studies.

The study of the technical characteristics of the CoI survey (Spanish version) supports its use as an instrument of measurement in educational research. The construct validity through the exploratory factor analysis allows to identify the teaching, social and cognitive presences, according to the theoretical basis that sustains the instrument. On the other hand, the results of the analysis of the internal consistency show a high reliability.

EXPANDING THE BOUNDARIES OF SERVICE-LEARNING AT HIGHER EDUCATION THROUGH E-LEARNING SCENARIOS: LESSONS FROM TEACHING INNOVATION PROJECTS

Amalia Creus, Mirela Fiori, Nadja Gmelch, Pastora Martinez, Universitat Oberta de Catalunya, Spain

Service-learning can be defined as a pedagogical approach that attempts to integrate community service in the academic curriculum. Through service-learning, students engage in organised activities designed to meet community needs and, at the same time, enhance their intellectual, social, and ethical development (Porter Honnet & Poulsen, 1989). Previous research suggests that participation in service-learning is associated with positive outcomes in different areas, among others attitudes toward self, attitudes toward learning, civic engagement, social skills, and also academic achievement (Blank, 1997; Billig, 2009; Conway et al., 2009; White, 2001). Studies on the topic also demonstrate significant increases in students' interest and commitment to their communities, and significant growing in leadership and problem solving (Creus & Lalueza, 2011; Eyler & Giles, 1994; Harwood & Radoff, 2009).

But even though service-learning has been deeply studied and is well recognized as a rich learning tool in face-to-face higher education, less is known about the challenges related to its implementation in an e-Learning context. Following this idea, this paper reports on the process and discusses the preliminary findings of two in-progress innovation projects that explore service-learning as a pedagogical approach in distance education.

The Universitat Oberta de Catalunya (UOC) is an online university whose mission is to provide people with lifelong learning and education by designing learning activities using advanced technological and communication resources. In this framework, we highlight the development of two specific teaching innovation projects, both designed from a service-learning perspective:

- Project 1: "L'Agència" is a virtual platform in which students have the opportunity to develop communication projects, experiencing authentic professional dynamics and issues. Moreover, they do so from a perspective of social commitment based on voluntary participation, as the projects are developed for free to non-profit organisations. This virtual agency was created in 2012 and since then more than 100 students have taken part in its activities. This teaching innovation project is being carried out in the context of a Communication Degree course that prepares students with the necessary skills to design, plan, implement, and evaluate communication projects.
- Project 2: Through "Participatory Final Degree" projects students have the opportunity of developing their degree or master final dissertation focusing on a specific social need of their community, and working in collaboration with a non-profit organisation or a social entrepreneurship. Departing from needs and challenges identified by different organisations, students are invited to develop research questions through a participatory research.

This study enables us to understand in depth the role that technology plays in shaping collaboration among the participants (students, teachers and non-profit organisations). Emergent results call our attention to the importance of moving the focus of the environment's design from the technology itself to the interactions generated by the users, who usually appropriate it in unexpected ways. It also addresses the importance of constant and progressive feedback as a key factor to ensure shared objectives and evaluation of results. This leads us to the need to further analyse the impact of the service-learning approach focusing on students' motivation and learning and also in its benefits from the participants organisations' point of view. Finally, the study allows us to identify the need to develop more flexible assessment tools and better methodologies to evaluate virtual collaboration in service-learning, taking into account the different levels of participation, social roles, individual expertise, and the ability of students to take cooperative decisions and manage conflict. These are some of the questions we want to address in further developments of our research.

HIGH IMPACT PRACTICES: ADDRESSING WORKPLACE NEEDS

Maureen Snow Andrade, Ronald Mellado Miller, Shaylana Davis, Utah Valley University, United States of America

Introduction

Employers have observed a gap between the skills they look for in recent college graduates and the skills these graduates possess. This has been noted in multiple studies involving both direct employer input and curricular reviews to determine alignment with professional standards (Association of American Colleges & Universities [AAC&U], 2013, Azevedo, Apfelthaler, & Hurst, 2012; Bayerlein & Timpson, 2017; Hart Research Associates, 2006a; 2006b; 2008; 2010; 2013; 2015; 2018; Pratt, Keys, & Tyrrell, 2014; Ray, Stallard, & Hunt, 1994; Ullah, Kimani, Bai, & Ahmed, 2018). These studies have also indicated consistency in the specific skills that employers value, typically written and oral communication, teamwork, ethical decision-making, critical thinking, and the ability to apply knowledge in real-life situations (Hart Research Associates, 2015). These are prioritized by most employers over technical or discipline-specific knowledge and abilities (Hart Research Associates, 2015).

Possession of these skills, referred to as cross-cutting skills in that they are important across academic disciplines and professions, prepare individuals for lifelong learning as those who possess them have greater ability to re-skill or up-skill as needed throughout their working lives. This study examined the effectiveness of high impact practices (HIPs), or activities that require a "worthwhile investment of student time and effort" (Kuh, O'Donnell, & Schneider, 2017; p.9). HIPs are designed to help learners develop the cross-cutting skills needed for the workplace. Selected HIPs were implemented in a required course for business students at a large, regional, open admission university. The course is taught in multiple modalities (face-to-face, blended, and online). In particular, students in the online version of the course are required to navigate multiple forms of technology to collaborate as virtual teams as they learn together. The objective of the study was to determine the impact of four high impact practices – writing intensive courses, collaborative assignments and projects, community-based learning, and ePortfolio – in preparing students for their future professions.

Findings and Conclusions

A key finding from documents across delivery modes was workplace application of the concepts the students studied, which were the focus of their artifacts and the foundation for their recommendations in their community consulting project. Teams developed leadership and teamwork skills, specifically openness to different ideas and acting on feedback from peers and the instructor to set goals for improvement. "Each team member has taken on leadership in a different part of this semester-long project. Although we have a mix of formal and informal leadership styles, our dedication to lead by example has given us great success."

As teams evaluated their performance midway through the course, they determined changes they wanted to make and set goals. These included items such as changing roles, creating new roles (e.g., a polisher to revise the final artifact draft), assigning tasks differently, starting tasks earlier, meeting earlier in the week, responding more promptly to communications, and adhering to deadlines. They also identified ways to improve accountability. "If a member of the group doesn't have their piece of the artifact completed by the group-proposed deadline, then it won't be included."

Teams also demonstrated that they were progressing through the stages of team formation to achieve the performing stage (Tuckman, 1965; Tuckman & Jensen, 1977). "Our team comradery has come a long way since the beginning. Every time we meet as a group, we get more comfortable with each other. This helps with sharing ideas because no one is afraid that if they say something it will get shut down."

In other cases, the teams demonstrated effective communication skills. "We all agreed that our biggest strength has been communication. Communication was the first topic of our team charter which was created the first week. We made it our goal to keep a constant open line of communication through group text messaging.

Overall, the analysis indicated that students were gaining the cross-cutting skills desired by employees through the high impact practices implemented in the course. In particular, application of the content studied to the real-world, particularly to students' own teamwork and to their consulting projects, communication, and teamwork skills were evident.

SENDING ONLINE TRAINING CONCEPT – COMPETENCY-BASED, ADAPTIVE LEARNING IN DATA SCIENCE FOR ICT PROFESSIONALS

Teemu Patala, ChangeLearning Alliance, Finland, Alan Bruce, ChangeLearning Alliance, Ireland

The European Union has noted over many years the existence of rapidly changing skills and persistent skills mismatches in the EU labour market. In the ICT sector, gaps have been regularly reported between skills required and skills actually attained by graduates of European Higher Education Institutes. The focus has been to adopt a more proactive learning policy that can develop and test mechanisms to help ICT graduates and workers acquire key relevant skills to make them employable and adaptable to future market trends. In addition, such mechanisms will be designed to enhance worker mobility and flexibility. The key steps proposed need to centre on engagement with employers to clarify their needs and with Higher Education Institutes to assess the nature of the skills, attributes and competences with which they are seeking to equip graduates.

Further issues identified in this process include; development of flexible learning modules to address identified gaps, piloting of learning modules in several countries, and evaluation of the impact of such learning modules from the point of view of ICT employers and workers. To achieve this goal, the "SENDING" project is developing two learning outcome-oriented modular VET programmes using innovative teaching and training delivery methodologies for two identified occupational profiles (data scientists and IoT engineers). Competitiveness, innovation and job creation in European industry are increasingly driven by use of new Information and Communication Technologies (ICTs) and the availability of high skilled and qualified workers in line with rapidly evolving market trends. ICT is a rapidly changing economic sector, with strong momentum and an important contribution to the growth of almost every economy. As ICT is a general-purpose technology, changes and disruptions in the economy can have significant influence on future skill demands for ICT professionals. Data Science (DS) and Internet of Things (IoT) have been recognized as the enablers among the key drivers of change with regards to the skills required by ICT professionals (Skills Panorama, 2016). Furthermore, Big Data and Data Science in general have potential to directly contribute €206 billion to the EU economy by 2020. However, one of the main barriers to achieving this potential is the forecast skills gap associated with Big Data given there will be a 160% increase in demand for Data Scientists from 2013 to 2020 for 346.000 new jobs. (European Commission, 2019).

The fact that stakeholders and beneficiaries of the project originate from four EU countries (Greece, Bulgaria, Cyprus, Ireland) characterized by diverse socioeconomic characteristics, VET systems and institutional environments is intended to result in project outcomes of broader European relevance and applicability. European cooperation among main stakeholders enables definition of a skills' certification mechanism with European standards, thus increasing the recognition of qualifications at European and national level within a sector, facilitating cross-border certification and building mutual trust. The "SENDING" training concept applies principles from competency-based learning, where the focus of learning is in concrete skills rather than abstract learning (Gervais, 2016). "Adaptive learning" (Ravindra, 2017) has gained popularity in corporate learning over the recent years. It refers to learning systems that adapt to learner-specific needs using automation and artificial intelligence (AI). Adaptation can make learning for workplace learners more targeted and can provide a better learning environment since learners perceive and process information in very different ways (Verdú et al., 2008).

In the context of "SENDING", training adaptation is made possible by using assessment before each learning module. The learning environment then recommends topics to be studied based on how the learner performed in the assessment. It remains to explore how much intelligence can be built into the system to make this process as precise, efficient and automated as possible. Thanks to the emergence of advanced learning data collection mechanisms and artificial intelligence (AI) there are new possibilities to develop online learning systems that enable more personalized and demand-driven training provision. This will be highly important in workplace learning environments where time-efficiency and return on training investment are always considered critical.

TOWARDS A PROTOTYPICAL CATEGORIZATION OF DISTANCE EDUCATION IN TEACHER EDUCATION

Andy Thys, Luc Vandeput, Jan Elen, University of Leuven, Belgium

Higher Education is in constant transition. In the Flemish context this is illustrated by a gigantic transformation in teacher education (TE). In the context of this transformation Educational master-level programs (EQF 7 – VKS 7) are designed and will be implemented in 2019-2020. The main factor that has to be taken into account is the a priori choice to offer the master programs at different locations throughout the Flemish region. This demands from the new educational masters in TE a radical focus on multi-campus education. This article stresses the need to establish a strong vision on distance education (DE) in TE. To do so a typology of distance education in teacher education is developed. Elen et al. (2014) can be seen as a prime inspiration for the different approaches (of distance education in teacher education).

At the core of this article are the three outlined approaches as a basis for discussion. A methodology is presented to systematically sketch this process and its future aspirations. It has to be noted that this search for prototypes can never be seen as a fixed description but as a constant search and debate.

EMBEDDING BLENDED LEARNING ENVIRONMENTS IN HIGHER EDUCATION: TOWARDS A EUROPEAN MATURITY MODEL

Katie Goeman, Stephan Poelmans, Veerle Van Rompaey, KU Leuven, Belgium, Wiebe Dijkstra, Willem Van Valkenburg, TU Delft, The Netherlands

The EMBED Project: A Quest for a European Maturity Model

The "European Maturity Model for Blended Education" (EMBED) is a higher education project led by a consortium of universities across Europe (this project has been funded with support from the European Commission). Aim is to support institutions when introducing, developing and implementing blended teaching (BT) and education (BE) in HE by means of a European maturity model or EMM. It includes criteria and instruments to assess the degree of maturity of BT/BE in a HE institution. It is conceived as a staged maturity model; it includes a framework for change, based on progress markers related to stakeholder-focused outcomes. The EMM is designed to assess BT and BE in terms of different levels of maturity, and to propose follow-up actions.

The EMBED Project: Status of Affairs

Conceptual and Descriptive Framework

A thorough literature review was carried out to get an overview on current conceptions, theories and models. The desk research resulted in a general conceptual and operational framework, the blueprint of EMBED. It includes the outline of key terminology principles on blended learning (BL), teaching and education (see also Goeman, Poelmans, & Van Rompaey, 2018). It allows researchers, practitioners and policymakers to talk common language and design, develop and assess current practices, strategical and implementation conditions in a systematic manner.

Design and Piloting of Monitoring Instruments

In parallel to the literature review, instrumentation for multilevel monitoring purposes was designed and piloted and a mixed-method field study was set up across the different partner universities. Objective was to understand in detail which BL environments are in place staff, which designs for BL designers and teaching staff in higher education adhere to (and why), and the way these practices are reinforced by the university context, i.e. the strategical measures and operational conditions.

Development and Review of the Maturity Model

The next step involved the definition of different levels, dimensions and indicators of maturity. For this purpose, a pre-Delphi study and an expert panel were conducted between December 2018 and January 2019. The current maturity model consists of three maturity levels, subdivided in dimensions and indicators considered crucial for discerning course and programme practices, next to institutional conditions and strategies.

Dissemination Activities

Throughout the whole project dissemination activities, including multiplier events and training initiatives, are organised on a regular basis. The purpose is to create awareness about the EMBED project, its progress and results (see https://embed.eadtu.eu/).

PROMOTING PERSONALIZED LEARNING DESIGN: THE ROLE OF ONLINE PEDAGOGICAL INTERVENTION

Hamdy A. Abdelaziz, Hamdan Bin Mohammed Smart University, United Arab Emirates

Online learning technology and design has maximized and optimized the potential of personalized, customized, and adaptive learning. This theoretical paper is proposing a new dynamic pedagogical intervention model for effective personalized learning design. This paper is an attempt to answer the following questions: (a) What are the disruptive learning principles of the third renaissance learning paradigm that impact pedagogical engineering and intervention for personalized learning design? (b) What is the suggested model for effective online pedagogical intervention to promote personalized learning design? This perspective was guided by ten emergent disruptive learning principles of the third renaissance learning paradigm that impact online pedagogical engineering, management and intervention for personalized learning design. Effective online pedagogical intervention has four major dimensions that are grounded/interacted and focuses on four metaphoric lenses: (a) types of learners (4Cs): Casual, Committed, Concentrated and Continuing; (b) pedagogical levels (4Ps): Intelligent, Agile, Distributed and Situated Pedagogy; (c) intervention levels (4Es): Enriching, Enhancing, Engaging and Empowering; and (d) online assessment frames (4As): Assessment of learning, Assessment for learning, Assessment as learning, and Assessment in learning.

HEARABLES: ELEARNING IN THE WORKPLACE

Rory McGreal, Athabasca University, Canada

Hearables are wireless smart micro-computers with artificial intelligence that incorporate both speakers and microphones. They fit in the ears and can connect to the Internet and to other devices; they are designed to be worn daily. One form of specialised hearables are the earphone language translators that offer potential in language teaching. This opens up the possibility of taking full advantage of these devices to support other forms of mobile learning in both traditional and distance education. Hearables can support the delivery of lectures, educational podcasts, notifications, and reminders through a wide variety of applications, while supporting interactivity. Intelligent hearables can determine the context and choose the right time and place to deliver the best content. These devices can become one of the principal ways we interact in learning and provide continuous support for independent, personalised, just-in-time, and self-directed learning contexts. Of particular interest to language teachers are the specialised hearables that serve as earphone language translators such as "Google Pixel Buds" and "Waverly Labs Pilot". This feature and others open up the possibility of taking full advantage of these devices to support language learning in both traditional and mobile formats including other forms of both traditional and online education. The capability of hearables for intelligent voice recognition (IVR) and natural language understanding (NLU) enables these devices to serve not only as translators, but also as powerful interactive digital advisers. In fact, these hearable interactions could become the principal means for spontaneous queries in any language. This has opened the possibilities for using IVR and NLU to support learning. With the availability of hearable devices, one can begin to explore in what ways, they can be advantageous in language learning. Hearing is a private and personal activity. This should be kept in mind when designing applications and tasks. Perhaps one of the most significant advantages for hearables comes with their ability to provide features that exceed the capabilities of the basic hearing aid. Hearables can augment the ability of the user to hear and discriminate sounds, helping the users to focus on those sounds that are the most important – super hearing, which can provide immeasurable benefits for language learners. For example, a student could be monitoring conversations in a target language. Hearables also facilitate switching from one function to another seamlessly, while providing useful advice as needed. With the growth of augmented reality and other forms of multimedia, users will need to have audio input, so hearables could become essential in these alternative language learning environments. In a mobile immersive environment, perhaps the most important application will be the ability of users to instantly access the information they need in real time.

CONNECTING STAKEHOLDERS THROUGH EDUCATIONAL TECHNOLOGY FOR EFFECTIVE AND DIGITALISED HIGHER EDUCATION ENVIRONMENTS

Christian-Andreas Schumann, Claudia Tittmann, Kevin Reuther, Helge Gerischer, West Saxon University of Zwickau, Germany; Feng Xiao, Oliver Schirmer, Tongji University Shanghai, China

Making better use of digital technology for teaching and learning, developing relevant digital competences and skills for the digital transformation and improving education through better data analysis and foresight, while still referring to educational policy goals such as support for high-quality education, developing Europeans' digital skills and making them more visible, boosting innovation and digital competences in all education institutions, opening up education systems, etc. (European Commission, 2018) Planning, implementation and control of teaching and learning processes are now linked to a digitized environment. The use of efficient methods, educational materials and modern technical media are expanded by the dimensions of digitization. International connections, relations to the future world of work places as well as community and individual social relationships are increasingly being intertwined in a digitized world and interlinked with the classic aspects of didactics, methodology and content.

Learning systems are combined systems with artificial (human-made), logical, informal, organisational and social impacts. Stakeholder theory means that organisations have obligations not only to shareholders but to other interest groups such as customers, employees, providers and the wider community, amongst many others. It is related to system theory, corporate social responsibility, and organisation theory concerning the role of cooperation in social systems and explanation of the behaviour in organisations and their environments. The Triple Helix concept describes the growing role of the social effects of universities in a hybrid system of university, industrial and governmental processes as well as their interdependencies and interactions in the knowledge society. The aim is to enhance the potential for innovation and business development through new institutional and social formats for the production, transfer and application of knowledge.

Following the achievement theory, the motivation of all stakeholders depends on their own condition as well as on the impact of the environment, whereby various dimensions, such as psychological, physical, social, etc., have to be taken into account. This complex structure is positively or negatively influenced by the technologization of learning through additional influences, which is expressed in a further dimension of "digitisation". If the behavioural approaches are now linked to the stakeholder theory, then not only classical relationships to organizations, management and leadership should be in focus, but also the aspects of the positive motivation based on corporate social responsibility and ethical behaviour under the conditions of digitization and technologization.

Stakeholders should be provided with a framework in which motivating conditions for the joint, successful development of educational technologies exist in a digitized learning and cooperation environment. The main issues are skills gaps, low return on investment (ROI), and the need for innovation, entrepreneurship, and job creation. That means strengthening the skills, increasing education´s ROI, and enabling all groups to be more innovative. The key aspects for the digital education are integrated digital education ecosystems, integrated learning life cycle, integrated technology solutions, as well as an effective and motivating environment. Stakeholders and their groups form communities for special target groups and application areas, which use the new technological and media possibilities to come together in connected education systems. In order to be able to successfully carry out their diverse and variously interests and motivations as an association or as a network, both individually and in cooperation, they need technology-based and service-oriented connecting subsystems, especially with regard to the new learning environments.

The interaction of stakeholders in digitised education systems implies connecting through educational technologies according to a holistic approach, which results in a multidimensional model for the connections in different dimensions. International double degree programs and exchange semester programs were supplemented by online components and are offered in perspective online in parity to classroom teaching with the participation and support of all stakeholders. The existing workplace impact and experience through stakeholder connectivity is complemented by online learning forms and educational technologies such as distance internship. On the other hand, new educational offers in the field of digital transformation and industry 4.0 act as catalysts for the dissemination of new technologies with a corresponding influence on the increased use of new educational technologies and their connecting effect. New educational technologies are used, among other things, to further improve connectivity among learners and with stakeholders. Social media plays a central role. AI will have a growing impact on development.

MAAM PROJECT – HOW DIGITAL LEARNING CAN BRING LIFE INTO THE WORKPLACE

Elisa Vimercati, Francesca Cirianni, MAAM Research & Development team, Italy

Abstract

Moving from conflicted situation between one's own roles and life experiences to the synergy allows people to have greater awareness of their personal resources and to apply them in all areas of their lives. But how does this happen, in what way? How do people experience it?

This is the question and objective behind the MAAM project. The research uncovers how digital innovation can build new bridges between people's life experiences and the workplace. The research starts from the experience of motherhood, which is paradoxical in its nature – on one hand unleashes energy, strength and competencies in the woman, on the other hand it is often perceived as a condition of fragility (physical, psychological) and is not recognized as a bearer of skills at the workplace.

The MAAM project is scientifically based on theories such as role accumulation, positive spillover, generativity, experiential learning and enriches them with two original views: life-based learning, that postulates that life is in itself one of the richest learning sources, and transilience, a meta-competence that identifies people's ability to actively bring resources and skills from one life domain to another and vice versa. This is an *action-research* project, with the aim to investigate and simultaneously activate the development of personal resources and soft skills in people.

This objective is achieved through an innovative digital platform that guides the woman in a process of self-reflection and awareness on different topics: the relationship with her identity and her own desires; the caretaking experience with the child and other people; the ways of listening, observing and empathizing and the consequences towards herself, others and the environment; the dynamics of delegation and decision making; the discovery of own "superpowers" and the reflection on the changes taking place.

The research summarizes the results of the digital platform for the first 19 months and has been focused on mothers' experience. It has the aim of investigating the impact of motherhood on the personal development and the soft skills of the women, highlighting which resources are active, which behaviors are adopted, how women perceive their roles and deal with the changes that comes with maternity. This is part of a broader framework, which has been starting to investigate / activate personal development and soft skills in fathers and whose aim is to investigate how caretaking activities trigger people's personal development and embed them with soft skills that can be used in every area of life, including workplace.

FREE DIGITAL DISTANCE LEARNING FOR EMPLOYABILITY AND SOCIAL INCLUSION: THE PERCEPTIONS OF MIGRANTS LIVING ON THE MALTESE ISLANDS

Joseph Vancell, University of Hull, United Kingdom

Research question and methodology

Migrants travelling from Sub-Saharan Africa to Europe, by sea, often end up in Malta where they spend months seeking asylum and waiting to be settled in a permanent host country where they can live safely or financially better. Many also travel to the Maltese islands to enjoy its economic boom. Malta, like most European countries, has created an integration strategy that includes face-to-face cultural and language courses, as well as skills-oriented learning initiatives, that is, courses aimed at enhancing their integration and employability. Migrants, asylum seekers and refugees, however, encounter many difficulties in joining and attending such face-to-face educational initiatives, due their social and family responsibilities. The Malta Lifelong Learning Strategy thereby argues for alternative educational programmes, including those provided online. Similarly, the UNCHR looks at digital learning as promising alternative for migrants and refugees. This paper will argue for the introduction of free online distance courses which, the author believes, can better facilitate the access to education for migrants. FDDL initiatives can also reach migrants who are committed to a job, particularly when employed in SMEs and microenterprises and have little time to spend on classroom-based courses and can be cheaper and use less human and infrastructural resources. Above all, FDDL courses can reach migrants in their country of origin, or when displaced in another developing country, *before* they start their journey to Europe. This research therefore tried to answer the following question: can FDDL courses make learning more accessible and thereby enhance the migrants' employability and their integration process?

This qualitative study was based on a sample of 16 migrants who were either seeking asylum, whose request for asylum was rejected but could not be deported and were living in Malta for over a year, economic migrants and refugees. The researcher identified this sub-sample while working on a larger project that was investigating the impact of digital learning on workers in Maltese SMEs. The anonymity of the participants was maintained throughout the whole project and their right to interrupt their participation in the research was communicated to them. The average age of the workers that were interviewed was 26, with 14 male and 2 female participants. This sample was not representative since the extent of immigrants working (many of whom illegally) in SMEs was not known at the time of writing. All interviews were conducted following a semi-structured approach. Each interview lasted an hour on average. The interviews were conducted face-to-face, at sites chosen by the participants, in the English language, and were audio-recorded with the permission of the participants. The data was then analysed using Grounded Theory approaches, including the constant comparison method which created codes and categories grounded in the lives and experiences of the migrants.

Findings and conclusion

The narratives indicated that the migrants and refugees are familiar with smart technology. They use it to seek work and stay in contact with their employer, families, friends and acquaintances. Some also use technology to learn informally from social networking sites such as YouTube, Facebook and WhatsApp, for example, about their asylum application process. However, few were aware and/or used already available online distance learning courses. The interviews also indicated that migrants and refugees prefer approaches which are tailored to, reflect and use their specific needs, characteristics and knowledge, rather than courses designed through a top-to-bottom strategy. These approaches are also in line with the UNHCR's recommendations for delivering education in crisis and conflict situations. The data also indicate that the migrants were willing to join educational programmes, particularly if these helped them gain a better job, with a better pay. However, they claimed that participation in class-based programmes, would be challenging with their current employment, and lifestyle. They argued that they did not have the time to join face-to-face classes because their primary concerns were finding and keeping a good job (or jobs), and "making money". This study showed that FDDL can be a means of empowerment through knowledge and skills for employability – including language proficiency – and social inclusion. However, despite the potential of e-learning for migrants, asylum seekers and refugees, the study identified significant challenges for the development and implementation of FDDL. This includes a lack of awareness of online educational offerings, particularly in the country of origin of the migrants, from where they can start their integration process and enhance their employability.

DIGITAL LEARNING TECHNOLOGIES IN PROCESSES OF INNOVATION AND DEMOCRATIC CHANGE? – REFLECTIONS AND QUESTIONS

Elsebeth Wejse Korsgaard Sorensen, Aalborg University, Denmark

> *"Nothing influences our abilities to cope with the difficulties of existence, so much as the context in which we view them" (Zeldin, 1994)*

Innovation with digital technologies in formal teaching and learning processes with the purpose of educating learners to become global citizens suffers from inertia. In particular, when it comes to innovation with digital technologies within processes of collaboration and dialogue. It seems that digital dialogue in education utilized for democratic change appears a complex challenge to address. However, historically, new technological innovations have often been rejected. It takes a long time to become accustomed to new technology and to realise its advantages, let alone to be actively utilized (Castells, 1998). Regardless of attitudes towards technology in general, the arguments have been strong for preparing learners for a future in a society permeated with digital technologies.

On the collaborative and dialogic fronts, however, the challenges seemed more complex. While digital technologies seem to have led to enhanced collaboration between teachers (in terms of use and re-use of resources), the promotion of student collaboration has not been enhanced notably. This corresponds to the observation pointed out by the teachers that the integration of digital technologies has not led to a real change in practice and innovation in teaching and learning methodology or alterations of teacher authority, teacher-student roles and power relationships within the learning processes.

Why does it take so long for educational communities to assert the digital perils and potential and implement the digital communicative and pedagogic potential of education of technologies in ways that cultivate, support and enhance the quality of education in general - and lifelong learning (LL) in particular?

Well, on the one hand, innovative development is hampered by tradition. On the other hand, innovation does not primarily generate from research directed towards technologies and their virtues, but more often it appears as a result of the bottom-up processes of educators in their own practices – in other words, from the use context.

In the present context, while reflecting on the contradiction, several issues and questions come to mind:

- The first issue (Q1) concerns the weight, impact and assumptions of traditions and the resulting general inertia with respect to implementing digital educational technology in innovative ways (e.g. for the cultivation of learning communities of practice) in the educational system.
- The second issue (Q2) concerns the ethical issue of "building" (general education) in a global educational perspective including: (a) the fostering of democratic citizens ("building" or socialization), (b) the promotion of ethical values, (c) the empowerment of the learners – with a focus on meta-learning.
- The third issue (Q3) concerns the pedagogical design of online learning architectures for the promotion of shared dialogue and knowledge construction.
- The forth issue (Q4) concerns teacher roles, innovation and learner-centeredness.
- The fifth (Q5) issue concerns the role of technology in processes of innovation and change.

This paper reflects on these issues, and discusses the various aspects involved. The structure of the paper and the discussions evolves around identified themes, and reflections on the issues and on their contextual premises are provided. The themes are: (a) The weight of traditions, (b) Educating ethically responsible and democratically empowered learners/citizens?, (c) The impact of pedagogic design decisions and meta-learning?, (d) Technology as vehicle in processes of innovation and change, and (e) Technology as vehicle in processes for innovation and change?

YESTERDAY-TODAY-TOMORROW: AN E-LEARNING PROGRAM ON MIGRATION

Bryan McCormack, YTT Association, France, Paola Perucchini, Maria Gaetana Catalano, Fridanna Maricchiolo, Roma Tre University, Italy

The present study presents an e-learning platform based on the educational programs carried out by Yesterday-Today-Tomorrow Association (YTT) and Roma Tre University. YTT is an independent Paris-based Educational & Humanitarian Non-Profit which combines visual language with learning tools to facilitate migrants' and refugees' inclusive processes, promote human-rights, the prevention of violent extremism, freedom, diverse, multi-ethnic and multi religious societies. YTT is also aimed at positively affecting national and international migration policy-making. Since 2016, YTT Association has been collaborating with thousands of refugees/migrants (from more than 50 nationalities, aged from 3 to 70 years old) in over 35 camps and squats across Europe/North Africa. They receive 3 sheets of paper and coloured pens and are invited to draw 3 sketches: one of their life before: Yesterday; one of their current life: Today; and one of their life imagined in the future: Tomorrow. These drawings define the YTT visual language, a raw, emotional and explicative language that speaks logically and directly to the audience.

Through drawing refugees/migrants express their thoughts and feelings independently of dialect, nationality or education and can leave their own trace, creating their own contemporary culture and voice, whereas simultaneously losing all traceability of their inherited culture. All of these drawings have been collected, filed, scanned and now makeup a digital visual database of thousands of voices, which is constantly updated with new drawings. They are used in the YTT educational program for pupils in primary schools using the YTT visual language to produce an imaginary contact with a migrant/refugee of the same age. The program aims to stimulate awareness of the living conditions of migrants and refugees, promote deconstruction of prejudice and reduction of discrimination practices, raising awareness among students to fundamental human rights and cultural differences. It uses student-centred strategies to activate empathy and perspective taking, creating a contrasting effect between their own experiences and migrants'/refugees' experiences, and to stimulate a deep emotional understanding of the migration experience.

A pilot study with 99 5th-grade children from five primary schools in Rome was conducted. Participants were distributed in experimental ($n = 56$) and control ($n = 43$) groups. Preliminary results show a reduction of implicit prejudice only in the experimental group.

Based on the research experience described, the e-learning program was created to provide a tool and a guide for teachers to utilize the YTT educational program. A learning platform is implemented which contains the teacher tool-kit, the YTT drawing database and other materials such as suggested activities, information, additional tools that could be combined with the drawings in the educational activities.

Currently, two programs are available: a two hours lesson and a five lessons program. For both versions, the e-learning program defines learning objectives, activities and strategies to realize them. The tool-kit is organized in an easy format so that teachers can download, print and use it to help realize the lessons. The YTT drawing visual database, organized as a catalogue, allows teachers to choose the refugees' drawings more suitable for their educational, social, cultural, ethnic context.

In the presentation, the core YTT e-learning platform features will be showed as well as the YTT educational and the pilot study conducted to verify its effects on prejudice.

THE INSTRUCTIONAL DESIGN OF AN ONLINE LEARNING ENVIRONMENT (RISSC) FOR UPPER SECONDARY SCHOOL STUDENTS' RESEARCH SKILLS

Louise Maddens[123], Fien Depaepe[123], Annelies Raes[123], Jan Elen[12], KU Leuven & KU Leuven Campus KULAK Kortrijk[1], Centre for Instructional Psychology and Technology[2], ITEC, KU Leuven, also at imec[3], Belgium

Abstract

In today's complex world, the acquisition of research skills is considered an important goal in (upper secondary) education. Consequently, there is a growing body of literature that recognises the need for well-designed (online) learning environments for effectively supporting the development of this complex set of skills. However, a clear consensus on how the acquisition of these research skills can be facilitated is currently lacking. Furthermore, interventions aiming to foster these skills are often implemented in specific domains, mostly in physics, biology and chemistry. In addition, current approaches to facilitation often refer to only a few scientific activities related to research skills. Because of the broad and (mainly) domain-specific character of research skills, the purpose of this paper is to articulate the instructional design considerations for an online learning environment for upper secondary school students' (broad set of) research skills in a(n) (underrepresented) behavioural sciences context.

Summary

In recent decades, the importance of the acquisition of research skills has been reflected in numerous curriculum and policy documents (Departement onderwijs en vorming, 2017; OECD, 2006; Opitz et al., 2017). These research skills should enable students to address problems in research, professional practice, and daily life (Opitz et al., 2017). Because of its broad (Fischer et al., 2014) character, it is necessary here to clarify exactly what is meant by research skills in this paper (presentation). While a variety of conceptualizations have been suggested in (recent) literature (Kestens, Elen, & Verburgh, 2016), such as scientific reasoning skills (Engelmann et al., 2016; Fischer et al., 2014; Opitz et al., 2017); scientific literacy (Norris, Phillips, & Burns, 2014) or research methods skills (Earley, 2014), in the present study the term research skills is used, as it adequately reflects the target concept as a broad set of skills (not merely referring to reasoning, literacy or research methods skills). Throughout this paper (presentation), the term will be used to refer to the definition suggested by Fischer and colleagues (2014), labelling research skills as a set of "skills and abilities to understand how scientific knowledge is generated in different scientific disciplines, to evaluate the validity of science-related claims, to assess the relevance of new scientific concepts, methods, and findings, and to generate new knowledge using these concepts and methods" (Fischer et al., 2014; p.29). In short, research skills include the knowledge and skills involved in eight scientific activities, namely: (a) problem identification, (b) questioning, (c) hypothesis generation, (d) construction and redesign of artefacts, (e) evidence generation, (f) evidence evaluation, (g) drawing conclusions and (h) communicating and scrutinizing (Fischer et al., 2014).

In this paper presentation, the instructional design considerations for an online learning environment aiming to foster upper secondary school students' research skills (in a behavioural sciences' context) are outlined. The online learning environment is called RISSC (Research In Social SCiences).

RISSC's systematic design is based on insights from instructional theory, with a main focus on the 4C/ID model (van Merriënboer & Kirschner, 2018) and the first principles of instruction (Merrill, 2002), and is unique because of its domain-specific focus on research in behavioural sciences, and its attention to eight distinct epistemic activities (Fischer et al., 2014). Although the models mentioned offer very specific guidelines, it is up to the designer to concretely operationalize these guidelines taking into account the domain under study. As such, more research is needed (and planned) into the validation of these instructional guidelines for the context of research skills in a behavioural sciences domain. These research plans will be further discussed during the conference.

EDUCATIONAL TECHNOLOGY FOR ACTIVE CONNECTIONS IN BLENDED LEARNING ENVIRONMENTS

Philip Uys, Charles Sturt University, Australia

This conference focuses on employing educational technology for connections. It assumes that these connections will be *active*, and not latent – otherwise these will be meaningless and ineffective. The emphasis is thus on creating effective learning environments. Such learning environments are not just online or digital, but can also be physical learning spaces in which educational technology can play a key role.

A key strategy to ensure that educational technology connections are indeed active is to employ educational technology within an active learning framework for both online and on-campus learning i.e. blended learning. Educational technology on its own does not lead to active learning – only when it is used within well-founded learning designs – of which constructive alignment is critical. Educational technology by itself is not "education's silver bullet" but should be located within "the essentials of teaching and learning: theory, pedagogy and emergent trends in the research". Such active learning will lead to learner engagement, leading to effective learning and learner success.

Learning spaces in the context of higher education refer to physical, digital and cognitive learning environments. The concept of *blended learning* acknowledges the above: learning, if not fully online, in many cases now occurs as a thoughtful blend or convergence of face-to-face interactions and online learning activities. The challenge is thus to ensure effective blended learning environments – not merely in purely online or purely face-to-face environments.

It is clear from the literature that learner engagement leads to learning and learner success. Active learning is "students doing things and thinking about what they are doing". It involves and engages learners in the learning processes which is opposed to a transmission approach. Active learning, fully supported by educational technology, is a key strategy to ensure learning engagement, thus leading to effective learning and learner success.

The above rationale can be depicted as follows:

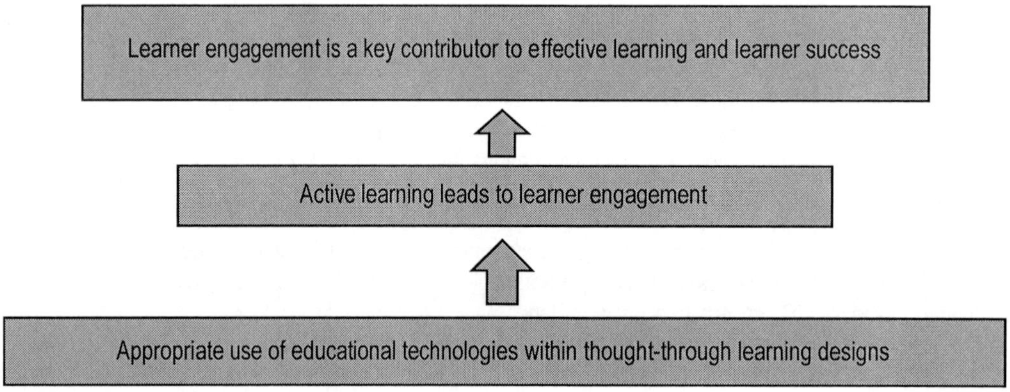

The fundamental precondition is that educational technology is employed within an active learning framework, based on the tenets of constructive alignment, thus leading to student engagement and ultimately to effective learning and learner success.

TOWARDS MATCHING ACCESS WITH SUCCESS: USING TECHNOLOGY TO CREATE AN EFFECTIVE LEARNING ENVIRONMENT FOR POSTGRADUATE DISTANCE LEARNING STUDENTS

Karin Müller, Marilize Putter, Milpark Education, South Africa

Distance learning has been identified as a key enabler in providing greater access to education. Yet, in order to provide meaningful access and constitute a productive application of both the student and country's resources, such access must include a reasonable chance of success. Historically in the South African higher education environment, the graduation benchmark on a postgraduate level has been set much lower for distance learning students than their contact learning peers, indicating that whilst distance learning may provide access, students studying in this medium have a much smaller chance of converting such access into successful studies. In this article, we reflect on the need to turn access into success for distance learning students, particularly on a postgraduate level and as it relates to financial planning students at a private higher education institution in South Africa.

More specifically the focus was on the Postgraduate Diploma in Financial Planning, which has been offered as a distance learning programme by the School of Financial Planning and Insurance of Milpark Education since its inception. Students study this qualification to obtain specialist knowledge in financial planning which spans fields as diverse as retirement, health, estates and wealth, asset management, insurance, employee benefits, law and tax.

Importantly, obtaining the qualification renders students eligible to write the professional competency exam of the Financial Planning Institute of Southern Africa (FPI) and upon meeting further requirements, to become accredited as a certified financial planner (CFP®). The CFP® designation is an international accreditation, and is regarded as the highest standard for financial planning professionals. Only six higher education institutions have been recognised by the FPI in South Africa as approved education providers. All other institutions other than Milpark Education's School of Financial Planning and Insurance are public universities; and of these, only one offers the qualification via distance learning. The access provided by the School via distance learning is therefore crucial in ensuring that students are not excluded simply by reason of the fact that they cannot attend contact-based learning at universities; and secondly, to increase in the number of candidates eligible to become CFP® professionals in South Africa.

Three years ago, the qualification was reviewed by the School, and the guiding question was how the qualification could be restructured in order to give effect to the call for meaningful access, and to address the factors that challenge distance learning students in their studies. In particular, the qualification was to be delivered in a new format, changing from distance learning to a distance learning online model, and it was considered how technology can be used to address challenges and create an effective learning environment.

In this article we review the changes that were made towards facilitating for success and specifically how technology has made such changes possible. We then review the initial results and feedback received upon the implementation of the new delivery format of the qualification. Although at an early stage, there are indications that technology has indeed served as a tool to alleviate factors inhibiting success amongst distance learners. The improved throughput rate, positive student survey feedback and the above-average performance of our students on the external professional competency exams are encouraging. While noting aspects that require further intervention for improvement as well as consideration and study in the future, there are indications that in respect of this qualification and the results achieved thus far, technology has, to a certain extent, levelled the playing field between distance learning students and contact learning students.

SELF-EVALUATION MANDALAS – AN INNOVATIVE AND MOTIVATING TOOL IN DISTANCE LEARNING COURSES (RESULTS FROM THE VTTPROJECT)

Peter Mazohl, University of Technology Vienna, Harald Makl, Pedagogical University College, Austria

This paper presents an innovative method of learners' motivation and self-evaluation in the frame of School Education. This method was developed between 2017 and 2018, has been evaluated in a case study in 2018 and has been tested in an international project in Austria, Italy, and Spain in the last twelve months.

Active learning using technology is a common way to achieve good learning outcomes. On the one hand, the pre-knowledge of learners is often unknown. On the other hand, educators should create strict and well-defined descriptions of the taught competences. Finally, the learning success should be evaluated. The self-evaluation mandala is an aid for all these important issues and gives learners the direct feedback – based on the learners' estimation – of the learning success.

Mandala is a graphic depiction which aims to increase the learners' control, satisfaction and, ultimately, motivation. It describes the taught competences in terms of knowledge, skills, and attitudes. The depiction or graphical pattern with the competence description enables self-assessment to take place at a regular pace throughout a course. This is done as a formative assessment, to provide *just-in-time feedback* as well as at the end of the course in form of summative assessment.

Pilot testing of the use of the self-evaluation mandala has been done in Spain, Italy, and Austria. This paper refers to the Austrian evaluation. The pilot testing took place in a typical grammar school that offers technology enhanced teaching (in the upper secondary classes). All learners use laptops (or similar mobile devices) based on BYOD (bring your own device). The pre-conditions for the testing were learners with a high level on digital competences. Besides that, all learners were common with learning platforms (in the case of the pilot testing Moodle ver. 3.6).

The self-evaluation mandala forces teachers to create a well-defined description of the taught competence in terms of knowledge, skills, and attitudes. Learners use the mandalas to get informed about their future learning and give a pre-learning feedback of their pre-knowledge before starting their course. Finally, at the end of the course, the learners give feedback about their learning success using the same mandala. The comparison makes their development immediately visible.

The paper explains the idea of the self-evaluation mandalas, their use and implementation in practical teaching in Austria This study is enhanced with learners from Italy and Spain in spring 2019. The final results (published at the web page of the project https://www.vtt-box.eu) present a study of the successful implementation in school education (with students at secondary high school level) and gives a first overview of the implementation of this innovative and motivation method in European countries. The evaluation was done by guided interviews to get as many individual feedbacks as possible.

This study was performed as a research part in the frame of the ERASMUS+ project "Virtual Teachers' Toolbox VTT-Box" 2017-1-ES01-KA201-038199 in the years 2018 and 2019.

CONSIDERATIONS FOR QUALITY ASSURANCE OF E-LEARNING PROVISION

Ebba Ossiannilsson, Swedish Association for Distance Education, EDEN, Sweden

Today's learning landscape is very different from what it was a few years ago. The way learners learn is changing dramatically. Today, learning is possible anywhere, anytime, and through any type of device. Mobile learning is the first choice for most people today. In the context of globalization and the knowledge-based economy, the quality of higher education is increasingly seen as strategically important for national economic development and competitiveness. High quality and relevant higher education provide students with the knowledge, skills and transferable core competences they need to succeed after graduation, in a high-quality learning environment that recognises and supports good learning and teaching. The combination of educational technologies is both natural and demanding, so quality aspects must be taken into account.

This paper is based on the European Association for Quality Assurance in Higher Education (ENQA) and its VIII. edition Report 2018 of the Working Group on Quality Assurance and e-learning. Reflections on quality assurance in e-learning, a report intended to provide guidance on how European standards and guidelines ESG can be applied in the context of e-learning. The recommendations of the ENQA paper apply to all forms of e-learning, i.e. earning achieved through the use of ICT, and indicators are provided to stimulate discussion between stakeholders.

In addition to examining the applicability and relevance of the standards defined in ESG 2015, the ENQA report is intended to stimulate discussion and reflection between the actors involved, e.g. universities, quality assurance agencies, etc.

Besides being based on the ESG, this report is based on the European Association of Distance Teaching Universities (EADTU) Quality in E-learning, E-xcellence Benchmarking framework. Furthermore, this paper is based on the presentations of the European Distance Learning Week (EDLW 2108) organised by the EDEN Special Interest Group on Quality Enhancement (SIG TEL QE) on 8th November 2018 on reflections on the quality assurance of e-learning based on this ENQA report. The challenges of quality improvement in e-learning need to be addressed at all levels, i.e. macro, meso and micro, covered in this paper.

A METACOGNITIVE MOOC FRAMEWORK

Jennifer Roberts, Ignatius Gous, University of South Africa, South Africa

MOOC completion rates are well documented as being very low, in most cases, between 5% to 15% (Greene, Oswald, & Pomerantz, 2015; Jordan, 2014). Many reasons have been suggested for the low completion rate. This paper investigates the thesis that one of the predictors of the low completion rates, is that students are not satisfied with the overall experience (structure, content, delivery, etc.) of the MOOC. According to the SERVQUAL measurement scale of satisfaction, service quality can be defined as the difference between expectations and actual experiences. The argument put forward in this paper is that service quality will be enhanced if students' expectation of the MOOC is well understood and that they are properly prepared for what to expect when undertaking the MOOC. This paper follows from an already accepted research paper featuring an autoethnographic journey of undertaking a MOOC. The author proposed a metacognitive MOOC framework, from a learner's perspective, based on her MOOC journey. In this paper, this metacognitive MOOC framework is examined in terms of reflective as well as practical components, to assist prospective MOOC students to be prepared for the experience and enhance their satisfaction with their MOOC.

The aim of this paper is to discuss the Metacognitive MOOC Framework proposed by Roberts (2019). The framework was developed to assist would-be MOOC students to better prepare themselves for the MOOC experience. The contention is that if students are well prepared and have realistic expectations, their level of satisfaction will improve. This could, in turn, lead to a higher completion rate of MOOCs.

The framework is based on Flavell's (1979) metacognitive principles of thinking about various aspects related to undertaking a MOOC i.e. thoughts about self, motivation and goals, the actual task and the strategy needed to complete the task. An understanding firstly of oneself – your own personality, and the related aspects of self-discipline and self-efficacy, organisational as well as self-pedagogical understanding, sets the basis for this metacognitive framework. Once the learner has thought about these aspects, then motivation and achievement goals need to be assessed. The framework places an emphasis on understanding your own motivation and the results that you wish to achieve through undertaking a MOOC – whether it be for lifelong learning aspects, an interest in a hobby, professional development or filling a knowledge gap. The framework then homes in to the actual task – in this case the MOOC, and prepares the student to think about the MOOC that they are intending to register for, to understand the content, the structure and the instructional design. Finally, the learner needs to comprehend the types of strategies that they are going to use to achieve their desired outcomes. These are practical questions related to time management, access to technology and digital literacy skills.

APPROACHES AND METHODOLOGIES TO SUPPORT CRITICAL REFLECTION

Jean Claude Callens, VIVES University of Applied Sciences

During their studies, pre-service teachers are continually asked to reflect. However, it does not seem obvious that students in teacher education reach a critical level in their reflections. According to several authors effective scaffolding of a reflection process encompasses a number of key features within cognitive and emotional domains. In this study we focus on cognitive features and search for an approach and methodology that may support a reflection process. There are different approaches and methodologies to support students to write their reflections. The number of steps in the different approaches to reflect varies from zero to eight. Some view the steps in a reflection process as sequential, while others contend that the steps of a reflective process do not need to follow any particular order. In this contribution, an approach that contains guidelines that may be considered sequential and step-by-step-structured is described as a linear approach to reflect. In contrast, an approach that does not include sequential, step-by-step-structured guidelines is described as a non-linear approach.

Besides variations in approaches to reflect, there are also variations in methodologies to support reflection. We distinguish in this contribution methodologies that are (a) primarily language based or (b) primarily image based and thus more multi-medial. The writing of a learning journal and digital storytelling may be considered as examples of respectively primarily language and primarily image-based methodologies to support reflection.

It is possible to vary the degree of structure (linear and non-linear approach to reflect) within each of the mentioned methodologies to support reflection (learning journal and digital journal). With the distinction between (a) the linear and non-linear structured approach and (b) primarily language and primarily image based methodologies to reflect 4 combinations are indicated (=linear and non-linear structured learning journal or digital storytelling).

Two studies were conducted. In both studies an experiment was carried out with respectively a pre-test post-test control group design and a post-test only control group design. In each study: (a) participants were student teachers, (b) the theoretical model of Kelchtermans was used to describe critical reflection, (c) the same procedure was used in order to determine the degree of critical reflection in the written reflection assignments, and (d) in both studies variations of the degree of structure (cf. approach to reflect) with respectively a learning journal and a digital storytelling were used.

The results in this study reveal that the mean score of all reflections on critical reflection is low. Second, a high SD is observed. Third, it seems that a linear-structured approach to reflect more effectively supports critical reflection than a non-linear structured one. Fourth, the lower score on digital storytelling (compared to a learning journal) can be explained by the idea that writing digital stories (or writing a comic strip) expects additional skills.

EXPLORING THE EMOTIONS OF DISTANCE LEARNING STUDENTS IN AN ASSESSED, ONLINE, COLLABORATIVE PROJECT

Jake Hilliard, Karen Kear, Helen Donelan, Caroline Heaney, The Open University, United Kingdom

Previous research has highlighted the importance of emotions of learners in online learning settings. However, much of this research has tended to focus on individual learning situations rather than social learning activities. The exploration of the emotional experiences of distance learners has also received little attention when compared to other student groups (e.g. full-time or blended learning students). As many distance learners are in full- or part-time employment or have other commitments, the emotions experienced and the reasons for these emotions might be greatly different to other student populations. This study investigated these issues by exploring the emotional experiences of distance learners when undertaking an assessed, online, collaborative group project. Self-report data about the emotions experienced and their causes were gathered using a structured diary at six times points during the group activity. Findings revealed that learners experienced a ranged of pleasant and unpleasant emotions before, during and after the collaborative activity. Feelings of satisfaction and relief were the most reported pleasant emotions and feelings of anxiety and frustration were the most frequently reported unpleasant emotions. To conclude this paper, implications for educators are briefly discussed and reflections on using an online diary to explore student emotions are provided.

DISCLOSING LEARNERS' BEHAVIOUR AND ENGAGEMENT INTO ONLINE AND BLENDED COURSES: CASE STUDY OF VYTAUTAS MAGNUS UNIVERSITY

Giedrė Tamoliūnė, Margarita Teresevičienė, Justina Naujokaitienė, Vytautas Magnus University, Lithuania, Josep M. Duart, Universitat Oberta de Catalunya, Spain

Interfaces between students' participation, number of submissions to discussion forums, attendance of online lectures and students' performance on their assignments are significant for students' success and achievements. Teachers' activities become more significant when delivering blended or online courses and their role changes from knowledge deliverer to learning designer. Therefore, teachers are challenged to recognize new learning behaviour models and find new ways to engage and motivate learners. Universities offering study programs in blended or online way need to recognize learners' behaviour, know how to analyse the data, make it 'understandable' to teachers and learners, and learn how to adapt course curriculum based on this data. Results of the case study conducted at Vytautas Magnus University revealed that after logging in to Moodle learning platform, students tend to spend time checking forums or course assignments rather than browsing another course content. Moreover, a significant drop-out rate was noticed after the 4th click, when 24% of students tend to quit the session. The results of this research confirm the fact that online learners' behaviour is changing rapidly, and teachers should be aware of that, understand preferred learning patterns and develop course content based on this data.

Online learning platforms like MOOCs and Moodle access and collect large amounts of data allowing to observe and analyse learners' interaction, behaviour and engagement into study process at macro and micro levels. When engaging in online or blended courses, learners have various intentions and experiences, and therefore they demonstrate different learning behaviours. To recognise learning behavioural patterns, teachers aim to master how to access the data, understand it, rethink course content based on this data and improve curriculum. Learning analytics help to understand and optimise learning processes and environments where this learning happens. Moreover, it could also help to measure learners' engagement, suggest study materials and resources based on test results, personalise learning experiences, provide feedback for the submitted work and encourages teachers' metacognition related to their teaching practice. LA serves as a metacognitive tool encouraging and allowing teachers to improve the way they teach and organise their teaching, helping students to learn and monitor their learning process.

LA can provide evidence of students' learning performance and behaviour in educational settings and consequently teaching strategies and instructional measures can be taken based on the presented facts. This also implies that such evidence will allow teacher to employ needed strategies and use personalized interventions as well more attention might be paid to low achievers. Learners' engagement in discussion forums and attendance of online lectures were found to be positively associated with each other, moreover, submissions to the discussion forums and amount of interaction online were directly related with a positive effect on learners' final exam grades.

These findings confirm that teachers' activities become more significant when both, recognising trends and challenges of learners' behaviour in online or blended course, or organising the learning and teaching curriculum by, for example, establishing a minimum reply requirement, drawing one's attention to others' ideas on a discussion topic, phrasing question in way motivates and engages as many students as possible All these transformations of teachers' activities demonstrate their changing role, from being knowledge deliverer to becoming learning designer.

Research results disclose, that when learning in a blended or online study courses, students demonstrate their need for an easily-absorbed information in small pieces. As data has shown, learners do no spend much time analysing course content, mainly focusing on the latest topic and news forum. For us, as researchers, this data analysis allowed to distinguish some aspects that our future research should focus on, e.g. how teachers apply LA data for their course improvement, do they recognise how this data should be monitored, what data do they monitor, and how they facilitate learners' discussions? To answer these questions, qualitative research will be conducted, providing a more in-depth and experience-based data on learners' behavioural patterns and teachers course organising reflecting these patterns.

Preliminary findings presented in this study will serve as a basis for further empirical research conducted in the four year-long scientific research project "Open Online Learning for Digital and Networked Society" (3.3-LMT-K-712-01-0189). The financial support provided by the ESF and Lithuanian Research Council under High Level R&D grant is gratefully acknowledged.

STUDENT PREFERENCES WITHIN A HOLISTIC BLENDED LEARNING ENVIRONMENT

Bernice Beukes, Karin Barac, Lynette Nagel, University of Pretoria, South Africa

Extant research shows that blended learning environments are widely accepted by students mainly because of the flexibility it offers. A thematic review on blended learning research highlights four broad themes which represent approximately 70% of literature published between 2000 and 2016 on blended learning. The most prominent theme identified relates to instructional design considerations (approximately 30% of literature). This stream of research, which include different perspectives on teaching models and strategies, best practices, implementation and environment matters, guidance, frameworks and the adoption of blended learning indicates that blended learning is becoming a common instructional model in higher education, while educators seek to integrate the strengths of both online and face-to-face learning and blend these two modes of teaching so that they become blurred and seamless transitions between them can be achieved.

Although the research on the instructional design of blended learning appears comprehensive, little is known about students' preferences within a holistic blended learning environment. Most previous studies have either focused on broad design considerations, differences between face-to-face and blended learning or have considered the effect of only one or two components in the blended learning environment. However, there is very little research that focuses on students' preferences within a holistic blended learning environment and the contribution that a component makes to the learning of the subject matter, especially in large class settings.

The purpose of this study is to investigate students' perceptions of blended learning components in a holistic blended learning environment and whether these perceptions vary for students with different academic performance levels. A mixed method approach was used in this study, performed at a residential university in South Africa in 2016, where a holistic blende learning model was incorporated. The holistic blended learning model included a flipped classroom (videos and lectures), weekly tutorials, an online simulation, peer-feedback and peer-mentoring. Students had to indicate on a Likert-type scale how they perceived each component in the blended learning model to contribute to their learning of the subject matter and an open question required students to explain further why they perceived the component to contribute to their learning. A response rate of 71% was obtained and the mean scores for the six component questions were calculated and ranked. The results indicate that auditing students do have clear preferences for specific components and significant differences exist between the preferences of different academic performance levels.

Such insights allow lecturers to adjust the resources allocated to the different components, and also identify activities which students might not perceive as valuable, but which contributes to the development of necessary 21st century skills.

EFFECTS OF ONLINE COURSE LOAD ON DEGREE COMPLETION, TRANSFER, AND DROPOUT AMONG COMMUNITY COLLEGE STUDENTS OF THE STATE UNIVERSITY OF NEW YORK

Peter Shea, University at Albany, State University of New York, Temi Bidjerano, Furman University, United States of America

Past research suggests that some students are at risk of lower levels of academic performance when studying online compared to students who take coursework only in the classroom. Community college students appear to be among those that struggle in online settings. In this paper, we hypothesize that online course load may influence outcomes for such students, especially those at risk for lower levels of degree attainment.

To examine this, we conducted a state-wide study using data from the 30 community colleges (n = 45,557) of the State University of New York, to understand online course-load effects on degree completion, transfer, and dropout. We considered three competing risks: departure from a 2-year institution for academic or other reasons (dropout); attainment of an educational credential; and transfer to a four-year institution. The focal variable of interest was exposure to online coursework, operationalized as online course load or the proportion of online credits attempted relative to all credits attempted in a given time interval. We controlled for both time-dependent and time-independent covariates.

Initial results, without considering all co-variates, suggest that students who opt for more online courses in any given time have a higher conditional probability of degree or transfer but, in this model, benefits wear off at higher levels of online course intensity. Conversely, this initial analysis indicates that increasing levels of online load decreases the hazard of dropping out in any given term to a point at which each additional credit is likely to result in increased risk for dropping out. Patterns therefore initially indicate a curvilinear relationship between online course load, degree completion/upward transfer, and dropout.

However, the curvilinear effect of online course load on dropout/departure can be fully attributed to course completion rates. In terms of degree/transfer, when course completion rates are accounted for, an increasing online load is linearly associated with increased likelihood of degree completion/ transfer. For a one-unit increase in online load, we expect to see about 72% increase in the odds of degree or transfer holding the remaining predictors constant ($b_{On} = .54$, $OR = 1.72$, $p = .008$). Holding other predictors at a fixed value, a unit increase in GPA translate into two-fold increase ($b_{GPA} = .70$, $OR = 2.02$, $p < .001$) and a unit increase in credits earned about an 11% increase ($b_{Cred} = .11$, $OR = 1.11$, $p < .001$) in the odds of degree/ transfer.

To qualify findings further, we sought to examine if the effect of online load may potentially depend on demographic and academic factors. Therefore, as a follow-up, we probed all two-way and three-way interactions between online load and time-invariant and time-varying covariates in the context of multilevel logistic regressions. With respect to the outcome departure/ dropout, the effect of online load is contingent upon GPA in any given time period and race (Caucasian vs. other). It appears from our analysis that online course intensity adversely affects the subpopulation of minority students who are academically stronger; these students are significantly more likely to depart/ dropout when the majority of their courses are fully online.

While some of the results reported here are good news for online students, certain subpopulations are at risk relative to the average. Of particular concern are academically stronger minority students; these students are significantly more likely to depart or dropout as their online load increases relative to other subgroups. Further study is warranted to understand the cause and possible interventions to address these issues.

A NEW APPROACH TO TEACHING INTRODUCTORY COMPUTING AND INFORMATION TECHNOLOGY BY DISTANCE LEARNING – ADDRESSING KEY ISSUES

Elaine Thomas, School of Computing and Communications, The Open University, United Kingdom

New introductory level 1 curriculum has been developed for the open-entry Computing and information technology (IT) degree programme in the School of Computing and Communications in the Open University (OU)(UK). Three key issues in Computing and IT teaching had been identified, namely: student retention, declining participation by women in Computing and IT modules, and the teaching of introductory programming at level 1. Dealing with these issues formed part of the rationale for developing the new curriculum. Computing and IT students at the OU are part-time distance learners and there is a diverse student population with a range of learning needs. Two-thirds of students are in employment, so it is important that their work-life balance is considered in the design of new curriculum.

Retention of students is an important issue in distance education (Simpson, 2012) as drop-out rates are high. Students study the new level 1 course TM111 "Introduction to Computing and Information Technology 1" first followed by TM112 "Introduction to Computing and Information Technology 2". Both module production teams engaged in a learning design process to assist with the management of student workload and to ensure coherence and consistency across both modules. The declining rate of participation by women in Computing and IT is a source of concern across both the employment and the higher education sectors (BCS, 2016). In developing TM111 care was taken in the selection of examples and images to ensure that female Computer Scientists were adequately represented so as to provide suitable role models for female students (Frieze & Quesenberry, 2019). Students often struggle with computer programming but easing "cognitive load" (Sweller, 1988) may be helpful, especially in a distance learning context. TM111 uses its own customised version of Scratch, called OUBuild, to assist students in acquiring foundational programming skills. TM111 is presented using a blend of traditional print materials with online learning and specialised software. The module is designed to appeal to a wide range of students with a variety of study intentions and learning needs, many of whom have few formal qualifications (or none at all).

TM111 has proven to be very attractive to students and participation by female students has increased to 24%, at least four percentage points over the previous module. Student responses to the module as a whole and to the teaching of programming has been very positive. More work is needed to evaluate the impact of the new modules in equipping students with the necessary programming skills to succeed with programming at level 2.

UNRAVELLING LEARNING ENGAGEMENT IN THE HYBRID VIRTUAL CLASSROOM

Annelies Raes, Pieter Vanneste, Marieke Pieters, Ine Windey, Wim Van Den Noortgate, Fien Depaepe,
KU Leuven Kulak, Belgium

Connecting learners and crossing borders through the hybrid virtual classroom

To deal with the current need for flexible learning trajectories giving access to a larger group of learners, the TECOL-project (https://www.kuleuven-kulak.be/tecol?lang=en) invested – among other learning spaces – in the design, research and development of a *hybrid virtual classroom*, as displayed in Figure 1. This project has been conducted in collaboration with two industry partners, i.e. Barco and Televic Education. The hybrid virtual classroom has been designed to connect both on-site students and remote students during synchronous teaching. Yet, an important question which we tackle in the imec.icon LECTURE+ research project (https://www.imec-int.com/nl/imec-icon/research-portfolio/lecture) is if this setting can satisfy the need for relatedness in the remote setting and how we can improve this satisfaction.

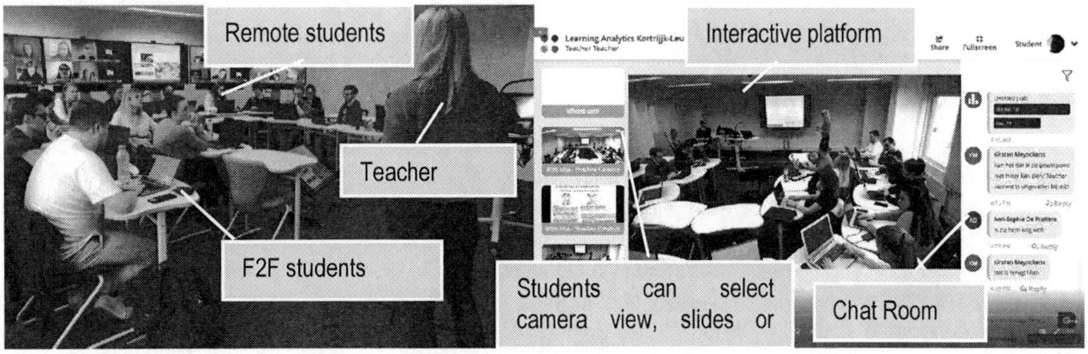

Figure 2. Left picture displays the hybrid virtual classroom including both F2F and remote individual students. Right pictures display the platform visible for the students.

Engagement of remote students from a self-determination perspective

The Self-Determination Theory (SDT) stresses that relatedness is a contributing factor for intrinsic motivation and indirectly also predicts learning achievement. Although there are numerous studies using SDT in various contexts, only limited studies used this theory to examine learning in the hybrid virtual classroom comparing different learning settings and its effects on relatedness and intrinsic motivation. The educational setting depends on whether students are physically present and thus follow the lecture face-to-face (F2F) or remotely (virtual), and on whether the setting is the same for all students (pure) or mixed (hybrid). This study presents the results of a quasi-experimental within-subjects design study comparing the students' learning experiences as F2F versus virtual student in the pure or hybrid setting. A mixed-methods approach is used including quantitative measures (i.e. real-time measurements of intrinsic motivation next to retrospective self-report surveys) and qualitative measures (i.e. an interview with the teacher and a focus group with the participating students).

Flexible, but challenging to learn in and to teach in

The results show that although the hybrid virtual classroom is promising regarding flexibility in education as it gives students the choice where to attend the course, it is also the most challenging one to teach in and to learn in as a remote participant. It has been found that both the relatedness to peers and the intrinsic motivation is the lowest in the hybrid-virtual setting compared to the three other learning settings. Future research should focus on how relatedness between the remote students and their on-campus counterparts can be improved by means of instructional interventions to improve students' engagement.

IMPROVING THE FINANCIAL KNOWLEDGE OF THE OLDER GENERATION – THE PLEKHANOV UNIVERSITY EXPERIENCE

Olga A. Grishina, Dinara R. Tutaeva, Alexey I. Grishin, Plekhanov Russian University of Economics, Russia

Older people in the modern labour market

It is not a secret that the level of social development of some certain society is not least of all characterized by the attitude towards the senior and older people. The problems and challenges faced by these groups of citizens have never been easy to solve, and in the modern world, they became even more complicated. Among the most relevant challenges is the accelerated development of technologies, above all – informational ones. Often, senior and older people are not able to adapt quickly to these changes. They not only experience problems in their daily life but also risk becoming "lagging behind", which puts them in a vulnerable position in the labour market, and often becomes the cause of personal psychological problems. This problem is particularly serious for countries with the *constructive* (or *regressive*) model of the population pyramid, which is characterized by the so-called "mound of the elders". Russia is among the countries experiencing this situation to the full extent. With relative stability (in absolute digits) in the number of working citizens of pre-retirement age, there is a steady increase in the number of working retirees.

What makes older people work

It can be said for certain that the main reason why older people continue to work is of a financial nature. In this light, the key task facing the society as a whole and the employer in particular is to help older workers overcome the fear of a subsequent life for an insufficient pension, that is, the fear of poverty. The results of the Silver Generation University (department of the Plekhanov RUE Distance Learning Faculty) activity allowed to formulate three main directions for solving this problem: ensure the employer's interest in preserving jobs for older workers, provide psychological support and enhance personal applied financial literacy of older people. The latter direction, being one that carry educational nature, was considered a priority for the Silver Generation University and required the development of special educational programs.

How to teach older people on a working place?

In developing the content of the relevant educational programs, it was decided to rely firstly on personal finance planning techniques, and secondly at acquaintance with various kinds of frauds in the financial environment in order to reduce the risk of becoming a victim. The pilot project was conducted by the Silver Generation University from September to December 2018. In total, 482 employees took part in the project. Within the pilot project, the following educational practices were used:

- On-line trainings. Special attention was paid to the structure of the information in the distributed materials, which was supposed to be quite intelligible, but at the same time maintaining academic integrity.
- Webinars organized before or after the workday. Given that the webinars have practically "lengthened" the working day, the organizers limited the length of these webinars to 30 minutes.
- "Live" (face-to-face) short-term sessions before or after the work day, as well as during the lunch break.
- Demonstration of short fascinating videos on financial literacy on TV screens installed in the CCOS canteens.

After the completion of the pilot project, a survey was conducted with the purpose of feedback receiving. According to the results, the audience as a whole was satisfied with the organization of the learning process. Wishes were expressed to increase the number of short-term "live" sessions, as well as to include in the program some basic information about the organization of small business and various forms of earnings on the Internet.

Thus, the experience of the Plekhanov RUE Silver Generation University shows that the highest effectiveness in solving the problem of increasing the financial literacy of older people may be achieved only by combining of educational techniques selected specially in regards to this particular audience's features.

PRECARIOUS VOICES: THE SHARED HOPES AND DREAMS OF THOSE TEACHING AND SUPPORTING LEARNING IN DIGITAL CONTEXTS

Peter Bryant, University of Sydney, Australia, Donna Lanclos, Anodyne Anthropology, LLC, United States of America, David White, University of the Arts London, United Kingdom

University staff in learning technology related roles are critical to the capability of the institution to effectively enhance the student experience, deliver an engaged curriculum and achieve significant pedagogical change. However, their perceptions of identity, precarity, status and capability and the locations and roles they are located within many institutions can challenge that capability. There is also significant variation in how visible or present University staff in teaching and learning related roles are in the integration of technology into wider strategic initiatives and how they understand or share their own sense of identity, either collectively or institutionally in that context (Browne & Beetham, 2010; Fox & Sumner, 2014; Walker & MacNeil, 2015). This places staff in these roles in institutional positions that can be rent with contradictions, often centred on where and how they act in supporting and leading technological change.

This paper draws on data gathered from an innovative series of workshops held in the United Kingdom, Australia and Germany in 2018 called Future Happens. These workshops involved a mix of invited and self-selected learning technologists, University management, stakeholders such as industry bodies and students and academics brought together to determine how they could be empowered and enabled to be the nexus between practice and strategy. The intention of these workshops was to encourage participants to be part of the discourse at their institution by generating, sharing and challenging the key messages, tools and strategies necessary to put the digital in the heart of the conversation with senior University management (such as the Vice-Chancellor).

As part of those workshops, over 200 learning technology related participants from 100 institutions were asked about their hopes and dreams of how they engage (or want to engage) with pedagogical and technological change at their institutions. Drawing on the analysis of the over 300 responses received as part of this activity, this paper explores the contradictions and paradoxes that impact on the capability of staff in learning technology related roles to influence and shape pedagogical and technological change. It identifies six key themes that emerged from the shared authentic experiences of our participants, including: Theme 1: Structural Institutional Support, Theme 2: Respect and Social Capital for Tech and Instructional Design, Theme 3: Integration of Teaching and learning into Technology, Theme 4: Confident Staff and Students, Theme 5: Digital Thoroughly Embedded across the whole institution and Theme 6: Digital Facilitating Transformation.

Some of the main conclusions of the paper are:

- At an institutional level, the responses highlighted that staff in learning technology related roles often frame the institution as a blocker, and themselves as an "outsider" (this can take many forms) rather than understanding the process of practice and culture change as the central task in hand.
- At a human level, how that change made them feel, how they learnt from it, how they located where the pressure or pain points were and how they understood their own reactions and emotions were critical underpinnings to the responses.
- It was demonstrable in the responses that our participants identified significant changes that needed to occur within their institutions which were not related to the purchase of a new piece of technology. They were pointers to some of the existential threats challenging their ongoing viability of their roles and more widely the notions of teaching and learning itself.

MASSIVE, PARTIALLY ONLINE CS1 COURSE

Tamar Vilner, Ela Zur, The Open University of Israel, Israel

The Open University of Israel (OUI) has an open admissions policy and is based primarily on distance learning. As in other universities, our CS1 course includes the topics recommended in the Computer Science Curricula (2013). The large number of students who register for the course (from 700-900 students per semester) presents us with unique challenges in management. In this paper, we describe the efforts we have devoted to making the learning and teaching process as uniform as possible for all students taking the course. We describe the research we conducted in order to ascertain whether there is a correlation between regular or intensive tutoring groups and student success in CS1 and whether the specific tutors affect student success. We were satisfied that the teaching of our course is quite uniform.

In the following paragraphs we will explain the factors leading to this result, and how we manage the course in order to achieve this uniform teaching process.

All OUI students enrolled in a particular course receive identical mandatory course materials at the beginning of each semester, as well as supplementary study materials found on the course website. The face-to-face meetings with tutors are designed to summarize and reinforce the information taught during the course. Although it is very helpful to attend these sessions, no extra topics or skills are taught.

At the beginning of each semester, students receive a timetable which details the syllabus, including which unit will be taught each week, and which assignments must be submitted. As a result, the course progression is unified at all study groups all over the country.

Before the start of each semester, a tutors meeting is held, in which we gather to discuss pedagogic issues. We share insights about the teaching process for this particular course, and discuss student misconceptions relating to the course which are encountered during tutoring sessions or in assignments, as well as solutions to the issues raised. The tutors share their thoughts about how to teach difficult topics and provide examples they use to demonstrate these issues. They collaborate to design good presentations which can be helpful to all the tutors.

During the semester, the tutors and the course coordinator keep in touch by email or in a special forum, to help each other solve problems which may arise that are connected to the teaching process.

Study centre teams are made up of mainly veteran tutors. Turnover is quite low, and most tutors are experts who remain in their positions for several years. Occasionally tutors leave and/or others join.

In order to make the assignment checking process as consistent as possible, we use this system: Each pair of tutors is given one exercise out of the eight assigned and are expected to prepare a guide detailing how to score the solution, how many points to reduce for each common error etc. The checking process includes two parts: (a) *machine checking*, which checks the correctness of the solution, and (b) *human checking* where the tutor reads the code and examines the programming style, the efficiency of the solutions etc. The guide prepared by the two tutors deals with these subjects as well.

Different forums are provided for students to ask questions about each exercise, and the two tutors are responsible for answering the questions in the forum, so the feedback is uniform for all students.

For final exams, the course coordinator, assisted by one or two tutors, checks all the exams of all the students. Prior to commencing the grading process, they meet to discuss the errors commonly expected, and how to grade the solutions. Each tutor grades the same question in all the exams. In this way, we guarantee that the checking process will be uniform.

REASONS FOR ATTENDING A MOOC: A SURVEY ON EDUOPEN LEARNERS

Annamaria De Santis, Katia Sannicandro, Claudia Bellini, Tommaso Minerva,
University of Modena and Reggio Emilia, Italy

In April 2016 the EduOpen MOOCs platform was launched in the Italian university context, created as part of a project also funded by the Ministry of Education, University and Research. There are over 50,000 registered users (April 2019) and up to now about 250 courses and 30 pathways have been produced by a network of 20 institutions.

The continuous development of the project involves the introduction of more structured initiatives – such as the activation of Professional Masters in MOOC mode, first in Italy – and the constant increase in the number of registered students. These elements require a reflection on the training needs, motivations and expectations of users.

A survey of 35 questions was subsequently conducted among EduOpen students to define demographic characteristics (first part) and motivations (second). In a broad research perspective, the analysis conducted will help us to understand the main uses of the portal by the students and to answer the following research questions: how to promote the continuous development of skills related to the human and professional expectations of EduOpen users in an open learning environment? What are the effective tools and strategies for rethinking the instructional design of the courses, starting from the needs and the opinions of the students?

In this paper we describe some results collected in the second part of the survey that determines the most interesting topics of study (categories) based on the opinions of the students and the reasons for registering in an open portal together with those for leaving the courses. The results are presented in relation to data obtained from the first part of the questionnaire (age, gender, level of education, employment and marital status).

The questionnaire has been answered by 6.6% of users enrolled when the survey was launched. To date, no sample significance testing has been conducted, but the high number of answers qualitatively supports the hypothesis that the sample is significant and representative of the whole population.

Summarizing the main results, we conclude that:

- the principal interests of EduOpen users regard Social sciences (53.9%), Computer and data sciences (42.8%), Arts and humanities (41.2%);
- the leading reasons for registration of EduOpen learners are to be found in a personal training needs (65.7%) and curiosity/interest in the topics of the courses (44.9%);
- an unsatisfactory interaction with colleagues doesn't represent a valid reason to stop attending a course (83.7%);
- the opinions of users about the navigation of the platform and the production of multimedia materials are mostly equally divided into critical and uncritical;
- the instructional design is an issue of interest for users enrolled in the courses: 54.4% of users will drop a course designed in an inadequate way. The term "instructional design" is not used as a synonym of active or collaborative teaching methods by users. In fact, the use of a transmissive teaching method is not considered by over 60% of users as a motivation to abandon courses.

These trends opened a discussion on online interactions among users and on profile of the EduOpen's Instructional Designers, technological tools and teaching strategies that allow to realize courses starting from the training needs of the learners.

BACK TO THE FUTURE, THE LEARNER STRIKES BACK: FEEDBACK AND REFLECTION AS KEY ELEMENTS IN MOOC RE-DESIGN

Conchúr Mac Lochlainn, Mairéad Nic Giolla Mhichíl, Elaine Beirne, Mark Brown, Dublin City University, Ireland

A general trend within research into Massive Open Online Courses (MOOCs) has been the study of learner behaviour and motivations using large-scale, quantitative studies to measure, correlate and predict forms of interaction and participation. Far few studies have focused on contextual, local and qualitative forms of inquiry, despite the great potential of such methods. In this paper, we discuss a preliminary study making use of qualitative data generated on an Irish language MOOC, namely learner comments on reflective steps each week. This data was analysed using an interpretive framework for elucidating both positive and negative forms of learner feedback. Three major themes are defined, relating to opinions regarding course materials, positive attitudes towards interaction and a broad metacognitive awareness of the process of learning. Implications for the design process and the importance of using such methods are briefly discussed.

MOOCS INTEGRATION INTO CAMPUS-BASED CURRICULA: THE CASE FOR RUSSIA

Tatiana Semenova, Ksenia Vilkova, National Research University Higher School of Economics, Russia

Massive open online course (MOOC) is a relatively new format of online learning; despite this, it is actively integrated into the educational process of universities. Using data from publications, regulatory documents of universities, official websites of educational institutions, as well as data from expert interviews, this paper summarizes the experience of Russian universities on MOOC integration into campus-based curricula. The main models of MOOC integration into the educational process were highlighted: (a) embedding the MOOC into the blended learning format, (b) replacing part of the offline courses of the academic program with MOOCs, (c) creating an online master's program with MOOCs.

Initially, the format of massive open online courses (MOOCs) appeared as part of blended learning technology to replace face-to-face lectures with watching videos outside the classroom with tests and quizzes (Hollands & Tirthali, 2014). Leading American universities began to create MOOCs by transforming and transferring their offline courses to an online environment. The practice of integration own MOOCs into the academic program has come along with the practice of buying a license to use the content of MOOCs developed by another university (Sandeen, 2013). Over time, the format of using MOOC in the educational process was transformed: MOOC was used not only as part of blended learning but also as an alternative to traditional courses. Since 2012, the practice of recognizing MOOC certificates has been taking shape, i.e. it becomes possible to get credits for MOOCs. At the same time, there are not only isolated cases of replacing traditional courses with MOOCs (Israel, 2015) but also the embedding MOOCs in the curricula as mandatory ones. Also, universities together with online platforms have started to create academic programs based on MOOCs.

At the moment, the question of the effectiveness of replacing traditional courses with the MOOC, as well as the creation of academic programs based on the MOOC, remains open. Despite this, MOOCs continue to be actively integrated into the educational process in foreign and Russian universities. It is believed that the MOOC integration into campus-based curricula allows applying and refining innovative methods in teaching in practice, improving the students' academic outcomes, bringing the effect of internationalization and co-studying from participating in the MOOC with different learners (Sandeen, 2013; Hollands & Tirthali, 2014; Belanger et al., 2013; Kizilcec & Brooks, 2016).

In this paper, we identify and describe the existing models of MOOC integration into campus-based curricula based on the research of practices accepted in Russian universities. For the description of the practices, data from publications, regulatory documents of universities, official websites of institutions, as well as data from expert interviews conducted with managers and employees of centres for online education at leading universities in Russia were used.

Models of MOOC integration into campus-based curricula in Russian universities

At the moment, three models of MOOC integration into campus-based curricula in Russian universities can be marked: (a) Embedding the MOOC into blended learning format; (b) Replacing part of the traditional courses of the academic programs with MOOCs; (c) Master's programs with MOOCs. The first model of integration is associated with the use of MOOC content in a blended learning format. Teachers can use materials of MOOCs created by their university, and/or by other universities, including courses in a foreign language, in their traditional courses. The second model of integration – the replacement of part of the traditional courses of the academic program with MOOCs, which can be implemented both at the individual and institutional levels. At the individual level, the replacement of the traditional course with a MOOC is an initiative of the student himself. In this case, a student can use not only the MOOC of his university but also online courses from other universities. Instead of a traditional course, students take a MOOC, which they choose from a list of recommended online courses, or independently. When the selected MOOC is not included in the list of recommended, the commission of experts evaluates the characteristics of the course and decides whether to add the course to the list. At the institutional level, the MOOC is included in the curriculum of the academic program, which students must pass it. The curriculum of the academic program may include MOOCs, developed by the teachers of both their university and another university. The third model of MOOC integration, which currently exists in Russian universities, is the online master's program. The first online master's program, devoted to the issues of modern combinatorics, was launched in the fall of 2016 in one of the highly selective universities of Russia. In our research, we highlight some conditions necessary to ensure the successful integration of MOOCs into the educational process of Russian universities based on data obtained from expert interviews. These conditions can be divided into three groups: (a) staff, (b) administration of the integration process, and (c) functionality of the online platform.

The first group includes university staff, tutors and assistants, who provide support for online learning and track the results of the educational process, as well as those engaged in designing online master's programs consisting of MOOCs from different universities. The second group includes conditions related to creating a transparent and flexible system at university, which allows using MOOC as part of the educational process and getting credits for it. The third group includes conditions related to the operation of the platform, whose courses are used in the educational process.

AUTOMATIC TRANSCRIPTION SOFTWARE: GOOD ENOUGH FOR ACCESSIBILITY? A CASE STUDY FROM BUILT ENVIRONMENT EDUCATION

Tharindu R. Liyanagunawardena, University College of Estate Management, United Kingdom

The use of multimedia has allowed the creation of rich learning experiences for students, especially for distance learners. However, the increasing use of multimedia in learning resources in higher education poses a challenge for learners with hearing disabilities, unless these are accompanied by transcripts or captions.

Prohibitive cost and extensive time requirement are major disadvantages of manual transcription. Automatic Speech Recognition (ASR) technologies have improved rapidly over the years, now almost in par with professional human transcriber in terms of Word Error Rate (WER) on accuracy. However, automatically generated captions and transcripts can sometimes fail to convey the meaning accurately; but for people with hearing-impairments this can mean inaccessible content.

This paper reports an analysis conducted at University College of Estate Management (UCEM), a leading supported online learning provider for the built environment, to assess the suitability of using automatic transcription software in the built environment sector subject disciplines. The following software were analysed in this study: Descript, IBM Watson Speech to Text (Watson), Sonix, Synote, Trint and Zoom.

A built environment specific text, containing 1000 words, was created for the experiment. The text contained subject specific terminology in the subject areas of property management, construction management, property and contract law, and building pathology. A purposely selected sample of 14 participants, all UCEM employees, with a range of native and non-native English accents, were invited to participate in the study. This small sample was selected to maximise the project's benefits, within the available time, by representing the diversity of UCEM staff and students. Only seven participants volunteered to create voice recordings reading the text.

Automatic transcripts were created for each recording. These were then extracted into Microsoft Word 2016 documents and pre-processed. Altogether there were 42 transcripts containing 42,000 words to be analysed. The Compare function available in Microsoft Word was used and then a manual colour coding was applied to identify substitutions, deletions and insertions to calculate the WER. As the final step, the best performing automatic transcription software's transcripts were presented to the subject matter experts to get their opinion of the automated transcript's quality.

The lowest average WER in this study was reported by Descript. Trint and Sonix came in second and third places respectively. Only few sections of two of seven transcripts created by Descript received "good enough" rating from subject experts as accessibility aids. None of the transcripts received a "good enough" rating in the subject discipline Property Management.

Accuracy of transcriptions is an important factor to be considered especially when they are used as accessibility aids. The study showed that the quality of the recording plays a role in how well they can be transcribed automatically. Though WER is used as a common measure of transcription accuracy, there are issues with this measure.

This study has shown that, although economical and timesaving, at present, an automatically generated transcript is not yet accurate enough to be an accessibility aid for the subjects relating to built environment sector.

SWITCHING CHANNELS: THE CHANGING ROLE OF VIDEO IN EUROPEAN UNIVERSITIES

Sally Reynolds, ATiT, Belgium/Media & Learning Association, Belgium

Most European universities have been using video as a teaching tool for many years. This includes not only the open universities for whom video production has been a stable component right from the start, but also more traditional universities, many of whom supported professional audio-visual production facilities designed to create high-quality educational teaching resources.

At the start, video in education was all about creating resources that could show processes and systems that were otherwise difficult to visualize. It was also about showing situations and contexts that were challenging to reproduce in normal university settings. University audio visual centres, were also charged with putting in place the services and systems to support the types of audio-visual support that academics required ranging from good audio in the lecture theatre to high-quality projection of images. These centres were usually the first to get involved in introducing the first video conferencing services and while the IT services also played a key role here, it was generally the AV staff who were charged with not only the equipment, but also with training academic staff in the use of video conferencing for teaching when this type of teaching became a popular way to reach remote campus locations and students in the 1990's.

Since then, the use of video for teaching and learning has virtually exploded and video technology for higher education has now become indispensable. Whether this is for the capturing and relaying of lectures or for application in high-end virtual reality scenarios, it is almost impossible to imagine a university setting where video does not play some kind of role. The introduction of student video assignments in assessment, the independent creation of knowledge clips by academic teaching staff, the use of subtitling and speech recognition to support access are all practices that place considerable pressure not only on university services but also on common practices and accepted standards within the university. At the same time AI (Artificial Intelligence) and Immersion look set to become common practice in higher education which raises questions that are not only practical in terms of cost but also ethical in terms of how far individual privacy is challenged by video based observation and assessment techniques.

Some of the issues that arise due to the increased dominance of video in university teaching are: How does a university manage the relationship for example between pedagogy and technology? Who decides on how and when new video based services are introduced? Managing quality and reputation is increasingly a challenge, how can a university best distinguish between materials that are created by and for the academic for use in his or her teaching as opposed to those that are created by a skilled and experienced audio-visual production team with a different set of objectives.

There is the whole discussion about whether video is being used to simply re-enforce what many consider to be the outdated one way transfer of knowledge model commonly seen in many MOOC and lecture capture settings, and if so, how can such uses of video be made more interactive and relevant to today's students. Synchronous virtual classes, with students fully engaged across all modalities are becoming common practice and systems to support learning and assessment in such environments are now possible. But what does this mean for academic teaching staff, how does this affect the process of learning?

For many of us the journey is only beginning.

ATTEMPTING TO REGULATE DISTANCE HIGHER EDUCATION: REFLECTIONS ON THE PORTUGUESE EXPERIENCE

António Moreira Teixeira, Pedro Barbosa Cabral, Maria do Carmo Teixeira Pinto, Universidade Aberta, Portugal

The continuous expansion in the use of digital technology to enhance teaching and learning experiences has led to a major shift in the Higher Education sector across the world. The large impact of new educational practices and forms of education delivery, as exemplified by the Massive Open Online Courses (MOOC) phenomena, has contributed to accelerate dramatically the digital transformation of Higher Education Institutions (HEI). As a result, an increasingly amount of distance and eLearning provision is now part of HEIs mainstream operations. In this new hybrid environment, the border between formal and non-formal education, as well as virtual and face-to-face becomes blurred. Moreover, the development of online learning has set new challenges to European and national regulation bodies as well as quality assurance systems.

Following the publication of the revised Standards and Guidelines for Quality Assurance in the European Higher Education Area – ESG (ENQA, 2015) specific quality standards and criteria have been developed in order to allow for European quality assurance agencies to appropriately evaluate eLearning delivered programmes (Huertas et al., 2018). However, in what regards regulation only a few countries have issued specific legislation on distance higher education and eLearning so far. The most notable cases being Italy and Brazil. These scarce experiences have generated mixed feelings on the part of the academic community. On one hand, the known examples prove regulation allows to assure transversal quality standards by imposing a number of minimum requirements which are mandatory for all providers. On the other hand, they impose strict rules and models which easily become obsolete in such a rapidly changing technological environment thus hindering continuous pedagogical innovation.

In Portugal, the discussion on the need for development of a specific legislation on distance higher education dates back from 2007. It was initiated by Universidade Aberta (UAb), the Portuguese open university, which is the major provider of online learning in the country. Being the dominant force, the institution feared that the entry of new players in an unregulated sector could lower the quality standards. At that time, a provision in the general legislation regulating HEIs has been made stating that a dedicated distance education act should follow up. However, this didn't happen. As all public HEIs started to provide distance and eLearning programmes, though, it became ever more apparent for most members of the academic community that some sort of regulation was in need. This understanding was shared by the national quality assurance body, the A3ES. The agency felt such regulation was paramount to provide them with a clear framework for evaluating distance and eLearning degrees.

In response to this demand from the stakeholders, the Portuguese Government has drafted a proposal for the Legal Framework for Higher Distance Education (Regime Jurídico do Ensino Superior a Distância – RJED). This is part of the Decree-Law nr. 83/2019. The RJED draft proposal presents a holistic view of how the sector should be regulated, combining a number of requirements for providers, programmes and courses and also a set of criteria to organize its quality assurance. Yet, it also imposes a new strategic ambition for the distance higher education system, by setting a target of 50.000 students enrolled by 2030. In addition, the RJED establishes a new specific role for the UAb within the HEI national public system. According to the draft proposal, the UAb should become the national research and resource centre for distance and eLearning. All other HEIs wanting to provide distance and eLearning are expected to partner with UAb for developing their programmes and courses. The UAb is bound to have all its provision delivered in partnership in order to receive public funding.

This new legislation has been submitted to public discussion in the Spring of 2019 generating significant controversy and wide criticism amongst the higher education system and the academic community. The focal point has been the combination of the regulation of the sector with a restructuring of the UAb mission awarding it a specialized role as a central hub in the distance and eLearning public higher education system.

In this paper, the authors analyse the RJED draft proposal, highlighting its most controversial aspects, as the limitations it imposes to pedagogical innovation and the specialized role it awards to UAb, and discussing the potential impact such regulations can have in the development of the higher education sector in Europe.

THE INTERNATIONALIZATION OF THE XXI CENTURY UNIVERSITIES: UNINETTUNO MODEL

Maria Amata Garito, Università Telematica Internazionale UNINETTUNO, Italy

After a historical analysis concerning the internationalization of Universities from the Middle Ages to today, the article presents the internationalization process of the International Telematic University UNINETTUNO, which has developed and continues to develop through two distinct models.

The first model is characterized by a new phenomenon in terms of modalities and speed, favoured by the diffusion of the Internet and online social networks. A spontaneous mechanism of global word of mouth, thanks to which in a few years the International Telematic University UNINETTUNO managed to enrol students coming from 163 different countries of the world, giving its identity a truly global character.

The second model is centred instead on international agreements with universities and ministries of different countries of the world and in particular of the Arab world, and is based on the involvement of the best teachers coming from the different partner universities, giving each of them the possibility to realize the contents of the different courses in their own language.

This has facilitated international alliances and the creation of new real and virtual spaces, in order to build networks of knowledge among the various universities of the world and to support the convergence of institutions.

UNINETTUNO, with its internationalization model, created a global network of public and private universities that bring together their knowledge, share resources and technologies, curricula, research laboratories, easily implement the mobility of teachers and students, while maintaining the specificity of the individual universities as a value and enrichment of the network.

CAPACITY BUILDING FOR VIRTUAL LEARNING INNOVATIVE TEACHING AND LEARNING IN JORDAN – EXPERIENCES OF JOVITAL

Katherine Wimpenny, Arinola Adefila, Alun DeWinter, Coventry University, United Kingdom, Valerij Dermol, Aleš Trunk, Nadam Trunk Širca, International School for Social and Business Studies (ISSBS), Slovenia

In a world that is increasingly interconnected, interdependent and diverse, engaging in international and intercultural learning and exchange is a key focus for the majority of higher education institutions (HEI). Such a trend can be considered in relation to several issues. For example, universities are experiencing an increase in their recruitment of international students; online international learning is increasingly becoming a core pillar of university collaborations for globally networked learning; and open courses such as Massive Open Online Courses (MOOCs) target learners, regardless of their geographic and cultural background. Many countries are experiencing, due to their demographic and socioeconomic context, a massification phenomenon concerning learners accessing higher education (HE).

Because of such trends, responsive, and effective education processes are required to maintain quality learning experiences. As an answer to the challenges mentioned above, state of the art education technology may be used in HEI to encourage learning as well as the recruitment of international students and the inclusion of students belonging to disadvantaged social groups. However, in some countries, restrictions regarding the amount of e-learning within study programmes can be noted. Such limits can also be seen as a rejection of e-learning methodologies as an inferior or lazy option where learning content is merely dumped online with little effort to contextualise the learning or to improve the learner experience.

In this paper, we outline how new and emerging technologies are being innovatively used in institutions around the world and on this base, how they are being adapted and implemented for use in Jordan. This includes applications of technology for domestic online learning, as well as global partnerships that develop intercultural competencies through the use of Online International Learning (OIL).

This paper presents the activities and the findings of ongoing the JOVITAL project in its goal of building the capacity of Jordanian educational technologies. JOVITAL is an international cooperation project co-funded by the Erasmus+ Capacity Building in HE programmes of the European Union during the period October 2017 – 2020 involving four European institutions and five Jordanian universities. The project aims to foster academic exchange using virtual mobility in order to offer learning opportunities to academic staff, university students and disadvantaged learners in Jordan. As it explores the world-wide state of the art in terms of education technologies, this paper outlines how new and emerging technologies are being innovatively used in institutions around the world and on this base, how they are being adapted and implemented for use in Jordan. This includes applications of technology for domestic online learning, as well as global partnerships that develop intercultural competencies through the use of Online International Learning (OIL).

Through presenting and exploring the activities and findings of JOVITAL, this paper seeks to outline the challenges and benefits of e-learning technologies in HE teaching and learning, and how these can be tailored for use within the unique Jordanian context. This paper argues that online learning, in many forms, is of benefit to students and teachers alike, but utilisation of technologies requires careful planning, tailoring, and training in order to see maximum benefit. As such, it is imperative that time is taken to train teaching staff and to prepare student expectations of online learning in order to gain the maximum benefit e-learning technologies have to offer. It is not merely enough to buy into technology and expects it to do all of the work – changes to approach and implementation are vital to the success of online approaches to pedagogy.

A NETWORKED LEARNING ENVIRONMENT FOR THE EDUCATION OF AN ARCHITECT

Melis Baloğlu Aşut, Yüksel Demir, Istanbul Technical University, Turkey

During a design process, a student of architecture learns how to communicate with various tools, understanding the problem and reflect his/her own solution and how to work together with his/her peers. To be able to examine how a student of architecture learn, communicate and act in a networked environment, this study analyses Theories of Architectural Design course instructed in Istanbul Technical University in Turkey as a case study in consideration of ACAD (Goodyear & Carvalho, 2014) framework. The course aims to examine all the dimensions of architecture, through essential "concepts", "questions", "problems", "texts", "works", "individuals" in unity. In this context, the interdisciplinary nature of architecture, the relations of architecture with "nature – culture", "art – science" will have the highest priority. All these studies will be realized considering the inseparable relation of theory and practice. An online assistant acts as an observer of the online platform of the course used as a case study, analyses the 14-week course according to ACAD framework.

As a conclusion, (a) students have been asked to reflect their ideas with different mediums so that they feel comfortable in one way and continue to use this particular way in their group project, (b) the community which can be defined as all the students who took the same course, needs to have a course memory to be able to continue to work together according to their changing interests. In that way, after graduation, students of architecture can remember the theory while heavily practicing, (c) During Theories of Architectural Design course, from 2003 to 2019, they have been using different platforms to communicate but none of them are designed for educational purposes. During architectural education, students share their design ideas in various forms. Current learning management systems fail in collecting files, storing them and sharing them. And also, in that tools, there is no room for custom design which can be another topic to study as a user interface design for educational purposes, (d) students can learn collaboratively by articulating and sharing their ideas while they are in universities, but they also continue to share their experience and expertise through discussion and dialog with the help of online communities after they had graduated. Lifelong learning communities can be constituted with the communities formed during the formal education based on shared interest and continue to grow.

As a final word, students can learn collaboratively by articulating and sharing their ideas while they follow their education if they have a chance to frame their own curriculum, and they also continue to share their experience and expertise through discussion and dialog with the help of online communities after they had graduated.

THE PRESTO PROJECT RELAY: OPEN, ASYNCHRONOUS LEARNING IN VIRTUAL PEER GROUPS

Pieter W.G. Bots, C. Els van Daalen, Sofia M. Dopper, Delft University of Technology, the Netherlands

Introduction

Academic education entails that students engage in open-ended assignments. Global education entails that students interact in projects with peers world-wide. The logistic challenge of offering academic project work to a large, heterogeneous student body, while keeping instructor workload manageable, is daunting. Faced with the challenge to provide students with sufficient individual practice and feedback, while at the same time keeping the teaching burden manageable, we have developed the project relay method and software (PRESTO).

The project relay method

The project relay was originally developed for teaching first-year university students the basics of constructing quantitative models. Since then, it has been adapted to support any type of project work that can be partitioned into consecutive steps, e.g., writing an essay (literature review → thesis statement → introduction → body of information → conclusion) or conducting a life cycle analysis (goal and scope → inventory analysis → impact assessment → interpretation).

In a project relay, students work in a virtual peer group on assignments that are organized in such steps. A student conducts each step on a different case/topic, building on the steps which have already been done by an anonymous predecessor. For each step, students have to (a) study the work which has been submitted by the predecessor, (b) provide constructive feedback and assess the work of the predecessor, (c) improve the work, and (d) extend the work by adding their "own" step. Specific rules have been designed to stimulate high quality work. Students work asynchronously and can perform the steps at their own pace. For a video explanation of the procedure, see https://youtu.be/SGm-DstdElk. The supporting PRESTO software manages the workflow of a project relay, and facilitates defining, monitoring, and grading. It has been programmed in Python on the open source platforms Django and Semantic UI, and is available under an open source license (https://github.com/pwgbots/presto).

Experiences with the project relay

We first applied the relay in the quantitative modelling course in 2013. In this course we have now run more than 15 relays with cohorts of over 200 first-year BSc students. The relay is also used in a first-year MSc course on policy analysis, and in 2018 we ran pilot relays in three different online courses on the edX platform. In addition, we have used the software in support of courses with "regular" peer review, as this corresponds with a relay comprising only a single step.

Our evaluations show that students learn a lot from the relay, and that this way of working provides a good way to practice. Students indicate that the workload of the relay is high. This follows in part from the effort of first improving one's predecessor's work before working on a new step. Students also find the relay quite stressful as there are incentives to provide critical reviews, but this is not always handled in a fair and constructive way by peers.

Conclusions and future developments

Experiences with project relays confirm that relays can be tailored to the subject matter and level of a wide range of courses, and that the PRESTO software performs well for relays with up to 350 students. The open, asynchronous, double-blind relay process and the web-based, LTI-compliant PRESTO software show good potential for implementing *virtual mobility*, as students enrolled in courses at different educational institutions could participate in jointly offered relays to develop generic academic skills by working in international virtual teams. The learning outcomes of the relay are good, but the relay can be stressful for students. We are planning to better prepare students for the review and assessment tasks, and we are exploring incentives for students to write more constructive reviews.

VIRTUAL LEARNING ENVIRONMENT FOR OPEN ONLINE LEARNING

Estela Daukšienė, Margarita Teresevičienė, Airina Volungevičienė, Vytautas Magnus University, Lithuania

Summary and Introduction

Digital networked society is learning in various platforms, in different ways and at selected time and pace. What are the preferences of members of digital and networked society for the learning platforms? What resources should be used to better fulfil nowadays learner expectations? And how higher education institutions are preparing for that? These are the main research questions of this research, which was performed with the theory analysis and quantitative research in Lithuania in 2018. The results of the research findings for the preferred learning ways and requirements for virtual learning platform of the online learners who speak Lithuanian are discussed in the paper.

Opening online courses for the society is more common in open universities, while traditional face-to-face learning universities focus more on bended learning approach and usually stay closed, mainly due to limited offer of open online courses. The use of virtual learning environment in university studies is also a common practice, but what features characterize open online learning environment – the virtual environment of 21st century learning of digital and networked society? Summarizing the theoretical findings on the features of open online learning environment the following categories were noted – easily accessible and stimulating learning, creating a community for communication and collaboration, and pedagogically well organized.

Research methodology

The aim of the research was to characterize open online learning environment in order to meet the digital and networked society needs. The case of Lithuania was selected for the research, focusing on the needs of digital and learning society for open online learning environment. The used survey method was mixed – combining online survey (the electronic version of questionnaire survey) and face-to-face survey (direct surveying at the respondent's home using multivariate stratified sampling). The total number of respondents, who qualitied for the digital and networked society description, was 1241. The main criterion to quality for the digital and networked society was the use of internet. Research participants' distribution by age was fairly even and ranged from 18 to 74.

Research findings

- The main research findings reveal that the most preferable ways of learning of digital and networked society representatives are distance learning courses with a teacher (their consultations and lectures) and short video tutorials or lectures with interactive tests. Respondents indicated preferences of learning content presented in different forms – written, video and audio; OER (readings and video recordings) to be used, learning material to be presented in small chunks and having clear instructions for learning with periodic feedback. The most preferable features of open online learning environment are:
  - the possibility to plan the time,
  - to be able to access learning materials, and
  - a possibility to communicate and collaborate with learners and teacher.
- Among least preferred environment features were the reception of badges, synchronized with virtual learning environment, which was, however, differently evaluated by younger and older participants. "A possibility to write a message" and "to connect in real time" is more important for younger adult groups.

More of the research findings are revealed in the full research paper and will be presented during the EDEN Annual conference in Bruge, in 2019. Practical application of the research findings and insights are integrated in Vytautas Magnus University Open studies platform (openstudies.vdu.lt), which focus on providing the university online courses for the community, and not just the university students. The theoretical considerations of the paper and further empirical research will be complemented in the further stages of a four-year research project "Open Online Learning for Digital and Networked Society (3.3-LMT-K-712-01-0189)". Project is funded by the European Social Fund according to the activity "Improvement of researchers" qualification by implementing world-class R&D projects' of Measure No. 09.3.3-LMT-K-712.

COGNITIVE LOAD DURING ONLINE COMPLEX PROBLEM-SOLVING IN A TEACHER TRAINING CONTEXT

Charlotte Larmuseau, KU Leuven Campus KULAK Kortrijk, Itec-Imec, Hendrik Coucke, Pamela Kerkhove, VIVES University of Applied Sciences, Piet Desmet, Fien Depaepe, KU Leuven Campus KULAK Kortrijk, Itec-Imec, Belgium

Online courses are becoming ubiquitous and increasingly tend to use authentic learning tasks incorporating real life tasks as the driving force for teaching and learning. Nevertheless, designing online courses that incorporate real life tasks is more challenging as these problems require more cognitive processes. This phenomenon can be explained by Cognitive Load Theory (CLT) introduced by Sweller (1994). CLT distinguishes three types of cognitive load: intrinsic, extraneous and germane load. The level of *intrinsic load* is assumed to be determined by the level of element interactivity. An element can be a definition, concept, formula and procedure that needs to be or has been learned. *Extraneous load* is mainly imposed by instructional procedures that are suboptimal, whereas *germane load* refers to the learners' working memory resources available to learn. The experienced cognitive load is mainly dependent of students' prior knowledge, but can also be determined by students' motivational beliefs. CLT research studies assume that sufficient motivation is required for participants to invest the mental effort necessary to meet the cognitive demands of the complexity of complex tasks. As a consequence, in order to design an online course for complex content effectively, it is important to understand how the different types of cognitive load are affected by students' cognitive and motivational characteristics during online complex problem solving.

Therefore, in the current study, a high and low complex task was developed in Moodle relating to the teaching of geometry within the mathematics course unit. Participants were 70 future primary school teachers. The complexity of the task was manipulated by increasing the element interactivity for the high complex task. To clarify, in the low complex task one element was questioned each time, and consequently students had to apply a single rule, formula or procedure (e.g., applying the formula of the circumference of circle). By contrast, the high complex task was based on a real-life context (i.e., teaching about the formula of the circumference of the circle), and had higher element interactivity as students needed to have knowledge of content knowledge, pedagogical knowledge and pedagogical content knowledge in order to solve the task effectively. Students could consult support while solving both tasks in the form of a manual and just-in-time information (i.e., hints). Consequently, in this context, students could take initiative in diagnosing their learning needs by identifying appropriate support. Since students could consult support, this self-directed learning strategy can also influence the perceived cognitive load.

Against this theoretical background, the aim of the study was twofold. First, we investigated differences in the experienced cognitive load while solving a high and low complex problem. Secondly, we examined whether students' cognitive and motivational characteristics (i.e., task value and self-efficacy) influenced the different types of perceived cognitive load, when taking into account the amount of consulted support for both the high and low complex task. Results of a Paired Samples Test reveals that the students indicate higher perceived *intrinsic load* for the high complex task when compared with the low complex task. This indicates that the manipulation of complexity based on element interactivity was successful. Additionally, results indicate that *extraneous load* was significantly higher for the high complex task. The difference in extraneous load could be the result of differences in students' self-directed learning strategies across the high and low complex task. Finally, results reveal a significant higher *germane load* for the low complex task, indicating that students found it easier to learn from the low complex task. A multivariate approach was chosen to assess the degree of interplay that may exist among students' cognitive and motivational characteristics and the different types of perceived cognitive load. Results reveal that students' self- efficacy has a major influence on the perceived intrinsic load for both the high and low complex task. This indicates that students' level of self-efficacy has a stronger impact on cognitive load than students' prior knowledge and task value. The consultation of support was also related to the perceived intrinsic and germane load for the high complex task, and perceived extraneous load for the low complex task. Due to the study design it is not completely clear whether students have consulted support to mediate their experienced cognitive load, or whether the consultation of support induced intrinsic or extraneous cognitive load. Follow-up studies should provide more insight into the direction of this self-directed learning process.

TEACHING GENERATION Z

Hristo Chukurliev, New Bulgarian University, Bulgaria

The article presents the experience of New Bulgarian University to create a training program for its academic staff to resume bilateral communication with students born after 2000. It examines the alianation of the faculty from the students due to digital technologies and the change in the perception of knowledge as a value and access to information. It presents results of a survey of the professors' opinion and presents a structure of a training program.

One of the main characters of the Generation Z is that it has been using the Internet from a very early age and has been working well with technology and social media. Other distinction is that this is the generation for which the internet is given. Thanks to the internet and the smart devices to access it, as well as with the help of search engines and Wikipedia, this is the generation for which information and knowledge are being pushed apart.

There is a distance between us and our students in their favour in terms of using technology and the Internet as means of completing immediate tasks. Learning how to do something, buying something, understanding what is something and what to do with it. However, this "information" does not turn necessarily into knowledge.

The need for action to overcome this gap between us and our students is obvious. From the collected information from the interviews we were able to distinguish 5 specific problems which construct the skeleton of the teaching program:

- *Motivation for learning.* Teachers are finding it increasingly difficult to keep student's attention on the material taught. The reasons for this lack of motivation for learning are different.
- *Visual information.* Classical linear text is increasingly difficult to understand for students as a source of information.
- *Theory vs. Practice.* Universities are increasingly preparing their students for the labour market rather than teaching pure science.
- *Evaluation.* A major problem to overcome in the learning process is the focus of the students on the evaluation and the grade they get rather than the learning itself.
- *Personal attitude.* In view of a growing lack of empathy in human relations, keeping the distance and at the same time the integration of students in a community with the teachers was the last important topic shared in the interviews.

The Generation Z is a generation that does not know the world before the Internet. This qualitatively different condition made Marc Prenski in 2001 call this generation *digitally born*, and the rest *digital immigrants*. At the same time, Prenski discusses how teachers should not train with "yesterday" and even "today" methods, but with "tomorrows". The options for this are two, the students to learn our language or the opposite. The answer will predetermine the future of higher and university education. And as if this question has already been answered – we must learn to communicate with Generation Z on its own language.

Universities face a complex and multifaceted situation where they must simultaneously make a number of transformations, often revolutionary, in teaching, appraising, and communicating, while at the same time preserving their mission in places where elite minds are grown and create knowledge. A positive side is that almost everything that needs to be done already exists and happens in one form or another. The challenge is how conservative institutions.

TECHNOLOGICAL RESOURCES FOR LIFELONG LEARNING OF TEACHERS IN THE DIGITAL ERA: AN ANALYSIS FROM THE LEARNING ECOLOGIES

Alba Souto-Seijo, Iris Estévez, Mercedes González-Sanmamed, Patricia Romero, Universidade da Coruña, Spain

Permanent education has become not only a requirement, but an unavoidable necessity to respond to the requirements of the school, as a precise change for the quality of teaching and teacher training. Thanks to technology, opportunities have been increased and forms and times to acquire the skills needed to function as a citizen and worker of the 21st century to have been extended. This framework has generated the concept of learning ecologies, which allows analysing the processes, mechanisms, and resources that a person has been generating in their life trajectory and of which they must continue learning. In this study we will focus on the analysis of an element of learning ecologies: resources. Understanding these, like those tools, with or without a technological base, that help teachers to develop professionally and stay updated. Thus, the main purpose of this research is to understand and reflect on how Primary Education teachers carry out their training and professional development, and what is the role of resources (personal and technological) in the configuration of their Learning Ecologies.

This research is of a qualitative nature. In addition, we must consider, that it is launched within a biographical-narrative approach. The sample of our study is composed of 5 Primary Education teachers from different public schools in the province of A Coruña (Spain). To preserve the anonymity of the participants and the confidentiality of the data, we have assigned them different names than the real ones. The data collection of the study has been carried out through an open-ended interview about learning mechanisms. This was made up of 71 questions, of which 25 related to learning resources used by teachers. In order to accurately record the interaction between the interviewer and the interviewee, a tape recorder was used. Then they were transcribed.

The method used to classify the data has been content analysis. Once the information was collected, it was distributed according to the units of meaning that were emerging. These units of meaning were labelled by codes that, finally, were grouped into thematic categories. As a guide in the coding process, we have elaborated a diagram of categories that helped us in the analysis process.

In this research, the results show that some of the participants learned to use technological resources in a self-taught way and others have introduced into this world with the help of their workmates. It should be noted that all of them use, to a greater or lesser extent, digital tools to facilitate the development of their classes. The difference resides in the possibilities offered by the schools in which they teach and the ability that each one has to manage with these tools with a certain skill. In addition, the five participants found positive the use of ICT, both to teach and to learn, but also reveal some negative aspects, such as the loss of personal treatment with people. Finally, in addition to technological resources, all participants highlight the importance of personal interactions in their training.

Acknowledgments

This study has been conducted in the framework of the research project (ECO4LEARN-HE), funded by the Ministry of Economy and Finance (Reference EDU2015-67907-R), and thanks to the funding received by one of the authors, Iris Estévez, in the FPI programme from the Ministry of Economy and Finance (BES-2016-077330).

INFORMAL LEARNING: CONTRIBUTIONS OF TECHNOLOGY IN A DIGITAL SOCIETY

Iris Estévez, Alba Souto-Seijo, Mercedes González-Sanmamed, Verónica Iglesias, University of A Coruña, Spain

Introduction

The digital revolution is causing continuous changes in different contexts, and education is one of them. Nowadays, knowledge has expiration date, for this reason citizens have to assume that training is not a one-time activity that takes place at a certain time, but that life consists of a continuous learning. This fact, perhaps, in case of teachers, has a greater importance, because they not only have the need to learn, but also the responsibility to teach in a changing environment. Different educational institutions must respond to the new challenges posed by the information society, but this formal education is not enough. Learning does not take place linearly or in specific spaces; nor can it be limited to the closed parameters of the formal training proposals. Nowadays, there are many possibilities to train and learn. For this reason, informal training models are becoming increasingly important, in addition to the classical formal training models. Based on this reality, the specific objectives that structure this study are (a) Identify which are the activities of lifelong learning, with or without a technological base, more frequent within the informal contexts of learning; (b) Study the reasons that cause the involvement of teachers in the informal-training activities.

Method

The sample consisted of 73 teachers of Primary Education of 11 public schools located in A Coruña, a city in the north of Spain. A 27.4% of the participants were men and 72.6% were women. In a 16.4% the average age is between 25 and 35 years old, 47.9% are between 36 and 50 years old and 35.6% are over 51 years old. In relation to their professional experience it should be noted that a 43.8% had between 21 and 35 years of experience as a teacher, the 28.8%, had an experience of between 11 and 20 years, the 13.7% had between 5 and 10 years of experience and, finally, 8.2% had an experience of fewer than 5 years.

The instrument used for data collection was a self-created questionnaire. The questionnaire was divided into 6 dimensions, although to carry out this study we focused on two of them. The first of these dimensions refers to the different types of informal activities that teachers carry out to develop themselves professionally, and the second is linked to the different reasons, which are behind the participation of Primary Education teachers, in this type of informal training activities. In the first one, thirty items are differentiated; and in the second, twelve items. Both have a Likert response scale from one to four.

This study, of a quantitative nature, is developed through a non-experimental-descriptive design. Therefore, to carry out the statistical analysis, it was used the statistic program SPSS 25.0. It started with an exploratory analysis, which allows us to evaluate the quality and distribution of the data (asymmetry and kurtosis), determine the summary measures (mode, media, and median), and calculate the dispersion measures (variance and range). In addition, we did descriptive and frequency analysis, in order to know the average score and percentages of each variable.

Results

The results show us, first of all, that the participants of our study do not prefer the activities based on technology to continue learning, it is still preferred the face-to-face training. It seems that the use of Technology for professional development has a fundamentally instrumental use for Primary Education teachers. In addition, it is assumed that they acquire the role of consumers of information, instead of producers of it.

The conclusion around the second objective of this study, point out the reasons behind performing of informal training by Primary Schools teachers. The results, we have obtained, show that teachers decide to involve in this type of training in order to be better professionals, therefore, to help their students, to innovate their pedagogical methods and to be updated. All this reasons are related to intrinsic motivation. Although, on the other hand, the reasons least valued by teachers for carrying out informal activities are related to the acquisition of certificates, or any kind of external rewards. Due to this fact, we deduce that, carrying out informal training is more associated with intrinsic motivation than to extrinsic one.

FINDING THEIR PLACE IN THE WORLD: USING DIGITAL STORYTELLING TO UNDERSTAND THE INTERSECTIONS BETWEEN STUDENTS TECHNOLOGY USE AND THEIR WORK, LIFE, PLAY AND LEARNING

Peter Bryant, University of Sydney, Australia

Understanding how and why your students participate in learning and the ways in which technology and social media support that learning is a key challenge for modern higher education institutions. Learning practices intersect personal, professional and educational lives in complex, inter-connected and personally defined and managed ways. How universities use information and data from students to ascertain and improve their experiences is central to most modern higher education institutional and policy frameworks on teaching and learning. However, much of the data collected through instruments such as student satisfaction surveys, national metrics for the quality of teaching and learning or other mass survey methodologies is argued to be contested, not reliable or aggregated so as to make insights difficult to isolate and interpret. The student experience is reduced to measurable and comparable numbers on scales and simple free text associations often only related to the delivery of unit at a single point in time. The student's story and how those experiences are related to other learning experiences in different units or their holistic experience of being at University can get lost. The challenge that student satisfaction surveys fail to address is how do we as institutions understand the collective experience of higher education?

Drawing on the analysis of digital stories told by 100 students at the University of Sydney Business School, part of the University of Sydney located in Australia, this paper will explore the unique methodological approaches of digital storytelling and student-led research to enhance how we understand the ways in which technology shapes and intersects the learning experience. It will also identify how students use technology (and especially extended forms of social media) to forms connections between their work, life, play and learning. The student's stories revealed varying states of transition, with the impacts of uncertainty, development, growth and reflection often starkly (and critically) described. These states of transition effected how they engaged with their learning and how they interacted with other students, academics and their discipline. Technology played a critical part in shaping and coping with the transition, acting as a both a catalyst for change and the balancing force between two uncertain states. The analysis identified three examples of these transient and uncertain states, aligned with dichotomous perspectives on social engagement and interaction, use of technology, teaching and learning, work and career and identity as a person and professional. What emerged were complex, intersecting narratives describing personal pathways through their work, life, play and learning. Whilst our students shared the experience of being in transition, there were significant differences in how they got here, how they coped with being in transition and how they planned their way out into more defined and stable places. There were also substantive differences in what role they saw for themselves, technology and social media, their academics and the institution in supporting, facilitating or challenging their transition.

FIVE YEARS OF KAHOOT! IN THE CLASSROOMS – WHAT DOES RESEARCH TELL US?

Matthias Murawski, Md Tawhid Hasan, Markus Bick, ESCP Europe Business School Berlin, Germany

One of the current major trends in education is the integration of innovative technology, and in this context, gamification plays an important role. In our paper, we consider one specific game-based learning tool: Kahoot! which has become the most played education-oriented quiz since its inception in September 2013. Given this relevance, there is surprisingly only limited and fragmented research on Kahoot!. We address this gap by formulating the following research question:

- What is the current state of research on using Kahoot! in education?

This research question is approached by a structured literature review. Our search efforts yielded 17 academic publications about Kahoot! in the context of education which we all analysed. For structuring our analysis, we considered the topic of Kahoot! in education as a socio-technical system with the three pillars technology (sub-categories: devices, requirements), human (learner, teacher), and educational institution (effects, subjects, purposes). These (sub-) categories were used to classify the foci of the selected articles.

We found that the focus of the analysed studies was placed on the dimensions: human and educational institution while, so far, less research efforts were put into technical aspects. Most of the articles put the learner in the centre of interest while only three out of 17 exclusively analyse the teachers' perspective. Also, effects of using Kahoot! are part of most of the papers (13 out of 17). Most studies are furthermore very context-specific, meaning that a concrete subject is considered. The purpose of using Kahoot! is hardly investigated at all. Regarding the research type, 14 out of 17 papers are of empirical nature. However, it must be noted that in most cases relatively small samples were collected and analysed.

Despite its practical importance and dispersion, our analysis reveals that research around Kahoot! is still in an early stage. This is firstly indicated by the very small number of academic articles dealing with Kahoot!. Secondly, existing articles place the focus on specific aspects of the socio-technical system while other also important aspects are neglected, which, in turn, paves the way for further research opportunities. This is especially true for technical questions around Kahoot!. For example, does the type of device (i.e., mobile, tablet, laptop) have an influence on the mostly positive effects of using Kahoot!? Also, technical requirements such as a sound internet connection sufficient even for large student groups or the availability of sound systems are hardly picked as a central theme. Regarding the educational institutions, there seems to be a kind of agreement on the effects of the use of Kahoot! which are generally found to be positive. However, differences between short-, medium-, and long-term effects have been hardly researched yet. Thus, future research could be focused on longitudinal studies to fill this gap. Also, the purpose of using Kahoot! is associated to interesting questions, but rarely exists in current research. For example, how could Kahoot! be applied or – if required – modified in the context of distance learning? What is furthermore completely neglected in research so far is the use of Kahoot! in companies, e.g., for training purposes. This topic seems to be highly relevant, given that almost all Fortune 500 companies use Kahoot!. Future research could start with case studies to explore related questions. Finally, considering the human dimension, we believe that more efforts are necessary to better equip the teachers with, for example, competencies to apply Kahoot! appropriately. In addition, scholars should try to generate more generalizable results, for instance, through studies with larger samples or cross-subject analyses. This would contribute to a better overall understanding of Kahoot!.

TEACHERS' AND STUDENTS' VIEWS ON THE EFFECTIVENESS OF TECHNOLOGY INTEGRATION INTO TEACHING AND LEARNING IN MUSCAT, OMAN

Adenike Adeyemi, University of South Wales, United Kingdom, Evdokia Pittas, UNICAF, Cyprus

Introduction

The aim of this paper is to discuss primary and secondary teachers' and students' perceptions regarding the effectiveness of technology integration into teaching and learning in Muscat, Oman. The socio-geographical context of Muscat, Oman allows us to examine the cultural change that is taking place with the evolution of technology with regard to teachers' Technological Pedagogical Content Knowledge (TPCK). In this paper technology refers to the multiple technological resources that teachers use in the school setting to support teaching and learning (Leask, 2013). Effective technology integration refers to the way technology is used by teachers and students to best support the learning process and achieve the learning goals. There are numerous and various changes related to the integration of technology as rearrangements and modifications need to take place in the daily school community life for both the students and teachers. Therefore, in establishing more general theories about the cultural revolutions with reference to technology, more evidence from different cultural and socio-geographical contexts is necessary.

Method

Participants were 44 teachers, 15 males and 29 females, and 219 students of grade six to twelve, 133 boys and 86 were girls. The data were drawn from two bilingual and two international schools in Muscat, Oman. The schools were purposefully selected because they share similar characteristics in terms of technology integration into learning and teaching. Oman has a centralised educational system meaning that the same curriculum is delivered in all schools (bilingual and international) across the country.

For this cross-sectional study, self-administered questionnaires with open-ended questions were administered. There were eight multiple questions, three open questions and one Likert scale question for the teachers and seven multiple questions, five open questions and one Likert scale question for the students. The research aim was examined with questions falling under three themes:

- Use of technology in learning and teaching;
- Technology competence;
- Perceptions regarding technology efficacy.

Conclusions and discussions

Results showed that both teachers and students enjoy the use of technology in teaching and learning and they similarly evaluate the effectiveness of available technologies. Although the majority of teachers agreed that teaching has become easier and faster with technology, only a small percentage integrates technology into teaching. Factors hindering technology integration concern curriculum design, network issues, time constraint and other.

Other important findings were the presence of newer technological applications such as ManageBac, Quizlet and Kognity which were available to students of the international schools. On the other hand, Social Medias (WhatsApp and Blogs) were not widely used by the teachers and students' participants as they were among the least indicated. Also, the lack of regular professional training did not hinder technology integration by teachers; the majority of them stated that they do not regularly get professional training.

In theory, the study contributes to our understanding of the reasons why teachers' and students' find it challenging to use technological innovations in school. In practice, the study provides educational authorities with suggestions on how technology can be used to support, enhance and extend the curriculum.

HOWEST EDHUB: THE INTERACTION BETWEEN DIDACTICS, LEARNING SPACE AND TECHNOLOGY

Basiel Bonne, Rina Dauwens, Tijs Verbeke, Howest, Belgium

Abstract

For many years, digital competences and working with computers have more and more become an integral part of the lives of people in our society. Banks close their bank branches and work online, cars become riding computers and our health is fully monitored. Nevertheless, in education, it remains very quiet in the digital field. However, ICT can actually strengthen education and teaching, but it still runs up against barriers.

Our research intends to fill the gap between existing technological applications and education practice and thus create space for the work field and the students to explore and experiment. To that end, we do not just put the focus on learning how to work with ICT or on tool-oriented workshops, but actually on the coherence between a thoroughly elaborated didactic scope, a flexible and inspiring environment/space and approachable technological adjustments to this space and the didactics. We investigate how we can achieve learning gains by making minimal interventions in the context or the learning process. We focus on in-class differentiation and investigate how the three quoted cornerstones – learning space, didactics, ICT – can facilitate teachers in the adjustment of their existing practice.

All of this is investigated in the field, in cooperation with our work field and our students. Because, they too want to experiment more with space and ICT and verify what works in their specific context. We work together in "Teacher Design Teams" in which the study department, the experts, the work field and the students work together to link space, didactics and technology as efficiently and as meaningfully as possible to one another.

In our session we want to share the current state of our research and our findings, and also introduce our course analysis instrument.

DESIGNING AND ASSESSING AN OPEN VIRTUAL MOBILITY MOOC: THE CASE STUDY OF THE "MEDIA AND DIGITAL LITERACY" MINIMOOC

Antonella Poce, Francesco Agrusti, Francesca Amenduni, University of Roma Tre, Italy

Introduction

The present work describes the pre-pilot phase of the Erasmus + project "openVM: Opening Education for Developing, Assessing and Recognising Virtual Mobility Skills in Higher Education". Virtual mobility (VM) stands for the ICT supported activities, organized at an institutional level, that produce or facilitate international, collaborative experiences in a context of teaching and/or learning.

The Erasmus + project is expected to achieve 7 Intellectual Outputs (IOs) related to different aspects of the Open Virtual Mobility ideation and implementation. The pre-pilot phase is part of the IO6 which concerns the design and validation of the OpenVM MOOC. The OpenVM MOOC is composed of 8 miniMOOCs aimed at developing 8 key skills related to Virtual Mobility: media and digital literacy, intercultural skills, autonomy-driven learning, active self-regulated learning, networked learning, collaborative learning, open-mindedness, and virtual mobility knowledge.

Methodology

The first miniMOOC designed is focused on the "Media and Digital Literacy" skill. The main topics of the course are: open education, open resources and licenses, the web mechanisms that could affect learning processes and media languages. Before starting the MOOC, the participants are required to fill in a pre-assessment. According to the score obtained, the participants are directed to the foundation, intermediate or advanced level. For each level, students need to read texts, e-books or pdf, watch videos and participate in discussion forums. Once they complete all the tasks, they need to fill in summative quizzes, write a post on their e-portfolios and make and receive peer-assessment in order to obtain a badge. The MOOC has a short narrative, by differentiating personas stories according to the user profile: teacher and student. The "Media and Digital Literacy" MOOC was first tested on January 2019 during the pre-pilot phase that approximately lasted two-weeks.

Analyses and Findings: the pre-pilot assessment

At the end of the MOOC, students were invited to fill in an online questionnaire aimed at investigating (a) participants' general evaluation, (b) participants' specific evaluation, (c) participants' recommendations for improvements and (d) hours spent to complete the course. Qualitative data from 9 participants were collected. 194 sentences and 259 segments were analysed through sentiment analysis using the software meaningcloud. The participants expressed positive sentiments related to the "Media and digital literacy" miniMOOC in 47% of the comments. The positive comments were related to the nouns "learning, topics, content, design, visual, videos, community" and the adjectives "simple, clearer". On the other hand, the negative comments concerned the nouns "the structure, e-test, e-portfolios, problems, task" and the adjectives "confusing, much, unattractive". The participants enjoyed the selected contents, especially videos. The basic level course (related with Creative Common) was the most endorsed. Although the participants appreciated the opportunity to test their skills through e-assessment and e-portfolios, they also suggested improving the e-portfolio functionality. The participants would need clearer instructions regarding how to fill in the e-portfolios, providing, for instance, a template. The participants have contrasting ideas about publicly sharing their thoughts during the discussion forums or e-portfolios. Whilst someone appreciated the opportunity to share their ideas with the communities, others did not.

Some participants affirmed that the text contents in the advanced level were too long and complicated and the instructions related to the exercises were not always clear. They did not appreciate being re-directed to external links, both for e-portfolio and for contents because they lost the track. It took 4 hours for the participants to complete the course: 60 minutes for the basic level, 90 minutes for the intermediate one and 90 minutes for the advanced one on average. Some of them completed the course within a week.

Although the general assessment of the course was positive, there is still room for improvements. Since DBR is an iterative process, the results of the evaluation of the pre-pilot phase will be used to improve the OpenVirtual Mobility MOOC structure. In addition, the results could also provide insights for institutions, educators and practitioners interested in developing Virtual Mobility at their own institution.

FLEXIBLE TEACHER TRAINING PROGRAM IN DISTANCE LEARNING

Sofie Dossche, Matthias Lefebvre, VIVES University of Applied Sciences, Belgium

Introduction

Our education institution can rely on 30 years of experience in distance learning. Throughout these years we have always considered the work-life balance of the students. One of our main targets is to establish a flexible organisation and an adequate coaching concept for our distance learning students. In this paper we present a number of factors which – in our opinion and based on our experience – can improve the success rate of study combined with work and (family) life.

Historical context

In 1997 University college VIVES (formerly known as KATHO) started providing an extended teacher trainer program for primary school. The program was designed to enable teachers, working in kindergartens, to obtain a certificate in primary school via a shortened study program. The aim was to try to eliminate the lack of primary schools teachers. In the beginning 7 students were registered. As they were working students the lessons were limited to Wednesday afternoons and Saturday mornings and the students had to study the course content autonomously. Back then, that was considered revolutionary. This training concept was often criticised. From 2002 on students could also obtain a degree in preschool teaching. The number of lessons were gradually dismantled and didactics through distance learning were increasingly developed. From 2007 on VIVES chose radically to support the concept of obtaining a bachelor in education through distance learning.

7 factors for a good work-life balance of distance learning students

We have listed up 7 factors which enable distance learning students to combine their studies with work and life. Based on our experience, we can determine these factors:

- 100% distance learning;
- Study program with exemptions;
- Flexible study program;
- Flexible exam schedule;
- Flexible teacher training planning;
- Coaching from a distance: quality study material and personal approach;
- Supporting the distance learning team.

Future challenges

Although we strongly belief that our flexible teacher training program helps students with their work-life balance during the studies, we are not blind for a number of shortcomings. In what follows, we present some challenges for the future:

- Dropout students;
- Procrastination;
- Collaboration with training schools;
- Collaboration with fellow-students;
- Personal follow-up of students.

THE INFLUENCE OF HIGH-FIDELITY PATIENT SIMULATION TRAINING ON SELF-CONFIDENCE AND STRESS IN NURSING EDUCATION

Sofie Merlevede, Birgit Vincke, Lisa Kerckhof, VIVES University of Applied Sciences, Belgium

Introduction & Aims

Previous studies have shown positive results regarding the use of high fidelity patient simulation (HFPS) within nursing education on several items such as teamwork and clinical reasoning. However, little is known about the effects of HFPS sessions on the perceived self-confidence and stress level of nursing students during their internships.

Aims

This study examines whether HFPS has an added value on perceived self-confidence and stress levels of first-year students of the bachelor program in Nursing during their internship.

Methods

First-year nursing students (n = 287) of 3 nursing schools in West-Flanders (Belgium) were assigned to an experimental and a control group. The experimental group will have completed HFPS before the start of their last internship, while the control group will not have received HFPS before starting their last internship. Instead, HFPS sessions are planned after their last internship. Both groups were questioned twice, after completing their first (no HPFS sessions for both groups) and last internship (experimental group: HFPS is planned before the internship, control group: HFPS is planned after the internship), using the self-developed questionnaire "Stress and self-confidence during internships". In addition, after each HFPS session, the Simulation Effectiveness Tool – Modified (SET-M) is used to estimate how students experienced their simulation session. The results are quantitatively analysed using the statistical software program SPSS.

Results

After the first internship and before HFPS sessions, first year nursing students score 6.78 out of 10 for self-confidence and 4.97 out of 10 for stress (1 – *totally disagree* and 10 – *totally agree*).

The students in the control group (n = 51) finished their last internship without receiving HFPS. The average scale score for self-confidence during their internship was 6.19/10 and for stress 5.25/10 (1 – *totally disagree* and 10 – *totally agree*).

The last internship (5 weeks) for the students in the experimental group is still in progress. However, the students received HFPS before their last internship. Based on the SET-M, the students reported a good experience with the simulation: The students scored mainly between *somewhat agree* and *strongly agree* on the statements of the SET-M. More concrete, the students agreed mostly with the categories regarding "Debriefing". The statement "Debriefing was a constructive evaluation of the simulation" scored the highest.

PONTE EN LÍNEA: A STRATEGY FROM DATA-BASED RESPONSE SYSTEM FOR PERSONALIZED LEARNING

Jorge León Martínez, Edith Tapia Rangel, National Autonomous University of Mexico (UNAM), Mexico

The implementation case of "Ponte en Línea" is presented. "Ponte en Línea" is considered a space for learning by presenting resources in a data-based response system for personalized learning. The categorization of the information included in this space is based on the organization and cataloguing of the so-called Support Units for Learning (UAPA by its initials in Spanish), which are mobile-based micro-learning tools (a widely accepted option for professional training) that have their origin in academic undergraduate programs. This program was implemented by the Faculty of Accounting and Administration (FCA) and the Coordination of Open University and Distance Education (CUAED), both dependencies of the National Autonomous University of Mexico (UNAM), for the benefit of the student population.

The UAPA exposes a theme through a didactic sequence and a structure made up of: Introduction (text that presents in a general way the contents, how they are organized, their relevance and suggestions for their study); Objective (the goal that the user will reach when concluding the study of UAPA); Content. (the presentation in different formats of the disciplinary, procedural or attitudinal knowledge that the user wishes to apprehend); Learning activities (work designed for the user to achieve the learning objective); Self-appraisal. (automatic evaluation with positive and negative feedback); and Information sources (references for the construction of UAPA). Due to its conception and structure, the UAPA can be used, reused or serves as a reference during different moments of the teaching and learning processes. In this way, the UAPA is an example of the so-called mobile-based micro-learning that in the words of Nikou (2018) "combines features of mobile learning and micro-learning to deliver small learning units and short-term learning activities". This is because UAPAs have the potential to support learners' autonomy to facilitate self-directed learning.

The implementation of the cataloguing for UAPAs required the initial effort of a group of librarians who defined the metadata scheme would be based on the Dublin Core Metadata Initiative. Subsequently, a revision of the syntax of the elements of the metadata schema was carried out. Finally, it was defined that the metadata would be incorporated externally, that is, they would be described in a database that would link to the referenced resource. In this way, it was possible for UAPAs to be organized and catalogued in the data-based response system for personalized learning called "Ponte en Línea". Data-based response systems for personalized learning provide materials appropriate to the level of competence of students based on the collection of information on use and search for them. Through analytical information, these platforms recommend playlists that give a different line of study to each student. Additionally, data-based response systems can allow users to share their playlists, so that they share their journey with their peers in case it is useful for someone else.

At the beginning of 2018, CUAED proposed the FCA a program for the creation of UAPA, for the second half of 2018, the FCA got in touch with CUAED to propose that through the UAPA, the hundreds of educational resources (in multiple formats) generated by the FCA itself over the course of 5 years would be organized. It was defined that "Ponte en Línea FCA2 (https://ponteenlinea.fca.unam.mx) was a program of the FCA, in collaboration with the CUAED of UNAM, to make available to students' various digital educational resources for use and reuse during their learning process. The proposal was accepted and the resources were organized under the categorization and cataloguing generated for the UAPA, so they would be accessed through them on the site "Ponte en Línea FCA". This is how "Ponte en Línea FCA" is organized by UAPAs from where you access other educational resources related to the subject such as digital notes, audiotexts and video lessons. The site was designed and implemented in Drupal, an open content manager, organized by categories in such a way that it could function as a data-based response system for personalized learning. In this way the student could access the resources through searches for keywords related to the subjects of his degree. "Ponte en Línea FCA" is also self-managed, and is available 24 hours a day, 365 days a year.

CONNECTING WITH STUDENTS IN AN OPEN DISTANCE LEARNING

Rodney Mabusela, Itumeleng Molefe, University of South Africa, South Africa

Abstract

This paper aims on exploring/expands mechanisms in which universities could utilize to connect with students studying in an open distance learning.

Introduction

The introduction of open distance learning has transformed the image of tertiary education globally. ODL has dealt with many challenges to learning that were experienced with traditional distance education, as it is more, practical, flexible and sometimes effective, particularly in an age of excess to connectivity.

Moore and Cearslely (1996; p.6) defined ODL as the distribution of learning materials to student who are specially distant from their lectures. Moore (1993; p.22) points out that it not merely entails a geographic separation by time. As the greatest portion of teaching and learning is realized outside educational institutions, it requires special educational and communication technology.

The implementation of information and communication technologies (ICT) has transformed the ODL university culture. There is a huge transformative in the way we teach and learn. Students are no longer passive listeners, but need to be able to do pro-active reading, encoding and decoding anywhere, anytime. In an online learning environment, students required to take greater responsibility in their leaning paths, and can share their vast of experiences and knowledge with others (DELA PENA-BAndalaria, 2007; p.12). Quality ODL requires interactive communication between student and lectures and other relevant support staff that is realized with the aid of modern ICT.

Effective communication is significant in human life, in education, where two or more individuals share information, knowledge, values, and skills, it is imperatives to communicate in such a way that any misunderstanding is avoided at all cost. with ODL this is the real challenge; to communicate effectively with students at a distance, in the third world countries, it is even more challenge to assist students to understand the expertations of ODL. The problem is that many students do not have access to electronic devices for online communication. Students who do have access to devices, do not always have access to connectivity such as internet access particularly when they should study off-campus.

Connecting with students is not an event which means it cannot be achieved over night, however it requires perpetual efforts to achieve it. Connecting with students means one must do the following: caring about the work-life balance of students, attentive to student's needs, expectations and the changing behaviour of diverse student populations including career, other studies, family life.

THE FOUR MOST COMMON CHALLENGES TO DESIGNING BLENDED LEARNING: A LITERATURE REVIEW

Ruth Boelens, VIVES University of Applied Sciences and Ghent University, Bram De Wever, Michiel Voet, Ghent University, Belgium

A comparison of challenges outlined by several influential studies on blended learning points toward the existence of four key challenges to designing blended learning: (a) incorporating flexibility, (b) stimulating interaction, (c) facilitating students' learning processes, and (d) fostering an affective climate. The aim of the present review study is to offer an overview of how studies on blended learning environments deal with these four key challenges. Starting from 640 sources, twenty studies on the design of blended learning environments were systematically selected for detailed analysis.

The research questions focus on how existing studies on the design of blended learning environments incorporate flexibility, stimulate interaction, facilitate students' learning processes, and foster an affective climate.

The results provide a comprehensive overview of how the four key challenges are resolved across the existing practices articulated in the literature. The major findings related to the four key challenges were: (a) only few studies offer learners control over the realization of the blend, (b) slightly less than half of the studies include support for social interaction, and when this is the case, social interaction is often stimulated through introductory face-to-face meetings, (c) much attention is paid to facilitating students' learning processes by, for instance, personalization and monitoring of students' learning progress through the online platform, and (d) fostering an affective climate is especially dealt with by focusing on students' motivation, while little attention is paid to appraising and dealing with emotions.

The present study offers a framework based on the four key challenges to designing blended learning and how existing blended learning environments deal with these challenges. This framework can help both practitioners and researchers to develop new blended learning environments, communicate about these developed blended learning environments, and assess existing blended learning approaches.

VALIDATION OF QUALITY INDICATORS FOR E-LEARNING

Dieter Maes, Marieke Metzger, Heidi Vanden Eeckhoute, VIVES University of Applied Sciences, Belgium

This study aims to identify and validate quality indicators for e-learning modules.

Background

E-learning plays an important role in education training for nurses and other healthcare professionals. It has a lot of advantages such as flexibility, high impact learning, cost-effectiveness. In case of quality care and accreditation it can be used as a new way of learning. Recently, a lot of different e-learning modules have been created and are available for care organisations. However, the quality of these modules cannot be guaranteed and care organisations do not know how to create good and qualitative e-learning modules on their own. A tool that screens the current e-learning modules for quality does not exist yet, but could help care organisations on their search for good and qualitative e-learning modules.

Methods

Firstly, a review of the most current e-learning literature was conducted to identify different quality indicators. Secondly, the results were discussed with experts to create a list of important quality indicators. Finally, the list was sent to a second group of experts who made a ranking according the degree of importance so that a final list of quality indicators could be derived.

Results

A list of quality indicators was created and divided into two categories: motivation and pedagogical framework (Table 1).

Conclusion

This study was important to define qualitative indicators for e-learning. Those indicators can be used to check current e-learning modules for quality so that healthcare professionals can keep on delivering good and qualitative care.

Table 1: List of indicators as a result of the literature review

Motivation	Pedagogic
Show progress	Learning goals (knowledge, skills, attitude)
Time (20-30'no longer than 2u+break) (possibility to stop in between)	Practice tests
User-friendliness (simple, easy to read, clear instructions, attractive)	Differentiation
Summaries + link to sources	On- and offline practice material
Well structured	Variety of educational material
Author is known	Feedback
Help function	New questions if somebody doesn't pass the test
GDPR proof	Interaction
	Learning content adapted to target group

HIGHER MOTIVATION AND SUSTAINABILITY OF KNOWLEDGE THROUGH SOCIAL MEDIA FOR TEENS

Nataša Rizman Herga, Andreja Kolar, Primary school Ormož, Dejan Dinevski, University of Maribor, Slovenia

The Use of Technology and Social Media in Natural Science Education

The objective of this work is to present the benefits of using technology and social media in science education. In the process of knowledge acquisition individual personal experiences play an important role. Individual research, experimenting, solving simple realistic problems, adapting to team and collaborative learning provides the basis for achieving valuable and cognitive objectives.

In chemistry and natural sciences in general the experimental laboratory work is one of the most effective methods for acquiring knowledge. A conceptual approach to teaching chemistry combines experimental work, problem oriented teaching methods and the use of the information communication technology with the goal to facilitate efficient learning and students' motivation on all levels of the learning and teaching processes. It is important to teach up to date content and connect it to everyday life. This way of teaching enables higher motivation for learning.

Methodology of Teaching Chemistry in this Case Study

How to educate students more effectively? By using "their" technology. ICT opens up a new educational world of creativity for students and teachers. Technology and social media can be used to promote students' engagement. They can foster student`s collaboration to work together, connectivism and media literacy. The most benefit in terms of learning will be provided when there is integration of technology and social media use in educational settings and student`s their everyday lives.

Students are instructed and partly guided to performing several tasks:

- Characterisation of the problem and collecting the information (research, study, plan...)
- Experimental work; Students discover the method of researching by firstly making the questions and then answer to them with experimenting. The teacher guide students which are writing the preparation to perform experiments. The preparation includes theoretical basis, the list of requisites, descriptions by steps of work, sketch of experiment or a picture of it and the explanation of experiment.
- Video recording plan; Planning includes writing the script, preparation of chemicals and requisites, division of labour, cover making and music choosing. After-effect is cooperation and team work building.
- Recording and film editing; Oppositely of watching experiments on television or computer, students are (by filming experiments themselves) on their own in the role of actors, cameraman, photographers and so on.
- Dissemination of the recorded video; Media sharing sites enable users to upload and share their multimedia content (photos, videos and audio) on the web. Using social media, teachers are able to improve the involvement of their students in studies and education, improve technological ability, provide a great sense of collaboration in the classroom and make good communication skills; especially if students feel affiliated and accountable to work.

Conclusion

A "case form" to make teaching and learning more effective is presented. By filming and editing a video, students are actively involved in the process not only with experimental work but also with technology. Using technology in the classroom improves engagement, knowledge retention, collaboration, creativity ... Students can also learn useful skills through technology (recording and film editing). Students are using Facebook, Pinterest, Instagram and other websites to socialize. We used their inclination by making learning enjoyable and effective. For dissemination of learning video they used applications they know. They popularized their work, knowledge, skills, chemistry, hand-on experiments... interest in learning natural sciences. Like? Subscribe?

THE ROLE OF MOTIVATION IN COMPUTER-SUPPORTED COLLABORATIVE LEARNING (CSCL) IN BUSINESS EDUCATION – A FOCUSED, NARRATIVE STATE-OF-THE-ART LITERATURE REVIEW

Carina Aichinger, Mathew Docherty, Sandra Mühlböck, David Kronawettleitner, University of Applied Sciences Upper Austria, Austria

Computer-supported collaborative learning (CSCL) is a pedagogical approach widely used in higher education, as innovative, active learning methods are constantly gaining popularity and the use of digital media in education spreading; distance and blended learning programs are on the rise. Motivation is recognized as an important factor in learning success and has been intensively studied. Still, there is no consensus on the influential factors on motivation in CSCL and a vast variety of research foci and study approaches exist. Therefore, the aim of this narrative literature review is to gain an overview and look into the current state of the art (2014 – 2019) of the role of motivation in CSCL, especially the influence of CSCL on motivation and influential factors (social, technological etc.) in CSCL on motivation. For this purpose, an extensive literature research was conducted online. Only articles from high-ranking journals were considered for the qualitative analysis, and the focus was limited on articles in the field of business education at the university/college levels. All selected articles were based on empirical studies. The findings suggest that there is a wide variety of different approaches and methods used in the research field of CSCL and they shed some light on what motivates people in CSCL and what does not, as well as which factors improve or hinder motivation. Due to the non-systematic nature of this literature review, generalizations on the role of motivation in CSCL cannot be made.

A SYSTEMIC MODEL FOR PERSISTENCE – A HUMANISTIC THINKING

Tomás Bautista-Godínez, Open University and Distance Education Coordination of the National Autonomous University of Mexico (UNAM), Mexico

Introduction

We propose a humanistic-systemic model of school persistence in Distance Higher Education as an opposite to instrumental models. In Mexico, as in other parts of the world, from an instrumental perspective, research suggests that incomes level, skin colour and other variables have a strong correlation among those who finish their studies. At the same time, persistence models, at least their representations, are generally shaped by variables and deterministic factors. Utopia, democratic dialogue between opposites and hospitality are elements we integrate in the humanistic dimension of the model, for the development of life through education.

Low persistence is a phenomenon that faces Distance Higher Education around the world. Persistence is the behaviour of continuing action despite the presence of obstacles. It is an important measure of higher education program effectiveness. Understanding of persistence phenomenon has been approached traditionally from deterministic approaches. Age, skin colour, ethnicity, incomes are some variables that constitute this kind of models.

A Humanistic and Systemic model for persistence

The humanistic category considers the next dimensions in the model of persistence: ethics, hospitality, and democratic dialogue between academy and students, as opposites. The main axis of our Becoming is knowledge (Bautista, 2019; Sánchez et al. 2019). This axis is into two vortices. One of them corresponds to utopia, the other to expectations. All this is immersed in an environment, which is considered an ideology.

The equidistant points between these vortexes constitute the exercise of introspection with feedback of teachers; that is to say, it is the own recognition and valuation of the acquired knowledge of the student and of the teaching practice. The environment as an ideology is a core component of the model because it alters our perceptions, of which we must necessarily become viewers and actors. Ideology, in this sense, is understood as a way of thinking that governs society as a whole. It determines social life forms and imposes a direction of life on institutions.

Ethics is associated with the value judgment on the decisions that the student takes to stay in the process of building through love, science, politics, and art (Badiou, 2016). It is the trace that the student projects and that, in turn, guides to the student. This guide keeps the student away from decisions about the nonsense actions and immediacy or alienation. It is an act for self-care and that of others. In Aristotelian terms, corresponds to the middle term. It is the point where the past, the present and what would have been converge. The imaginary time has been taken from the theory of creative evolution developed by Bergson (2007).

Hospitality, as a way of acting, metaphorically, opens the doors to the Other (Bautista, 2019). Allow the host to become the guest. It is a way of taking care of ourselves. It is the beginning of an emancipatory exercise through the knowledge that builds ourselves and we build it between academy and students. Through hospitality we show ourselves ethically. It is the form of the relationship established by teachers and students and the community as a whole. Hospitality becomes the condition of democratic dialogue. It allows us to detach ourselves from apathy and enables the exploration of the unknown in search of the resignification of oneself.

FROM IDEA TO IMPACT: A QUALITY ASSURANCE MODEL FOR MOVING DIGITAL INNOVATION TO STANDARD OPERATING PROCEDURE

Deborah Adair, Quality Matters, United States of America

Innovation is costly: Achieving impact at scale requires standardized practice

An innovation, even if "proven" elsewhere, requires significant organizational attention and energy. Learning, customizing, piloting, and refining all take time and money. What comes next however – dissemination, institutional adoption, and institutional practice – is essentially an organizational change initiative. An organization must be implementing the innovation at scale to realize the full potential – to see impact.

An organization can support only so many innovations at one time. They must free up time, energy, and resources by moving innovation into standard practice, so that the innovation becomes just the way to do business. Moving from innovation to S.O.P. makes way for new opportunities by releasing creative energy and organizational capacity for the next innovation.

Educational innovations must maintain the benefits for students as they are moved to SOPs. Innovations in teaching and learning must result in improved student learning and success as they are scaled and turned into standard practice. An effective tool to ensure both aims is to implement a robust quality assurance process.

A quality assurance-focused model for moving innovation to impact

For any educational innovation, the desire is to replicate and implement in ways that assure quality and achieve the desired outcome. A clear definition of quality in its relationship to the desired outcome is required to structure a quality assurance process that will eventually turn the innovation into a standard operating procedure. Unlike many nascent innovations, eLearning is a mature educational innovation and much is known about quality in online education. For online learning, there are well-accepted standards to follow in creating and delivering online education.

Such standards provide the core for a structured continuum or model for excellence in quality assurance to move from innovation to SOP. The most common starting place in this *Continuum of Excellence* model is with an *Ad Hoc* implementation of the innovation (e.g. online education) – with the goal of reducing resistance to adoption and other implementation barriers through a period of introduction and familiarization with quality expectations in the use of the innovation. Quality criteria are disseminated, typically, through persuasion and incentive and not put forward as a mandate.

The *Quality Evaluation* phase, the next step in the model, requires training on the quality criteria and putting in place an internal, structured, and periodic process to evaluate against the criteria. This is typically used only to evaluate what is/is not meeting criteria and is often used in a gatekeeping manner – allowing only implementations meeting criteria to move forward. The *Continuous Improvement* phase is a more robust way to modify and improve the implementation of the innovation – by measuring outcomes and analysing data, making changes based on it, and re-evaluating in a continuous process.

The *Benchmarking* phase requires an unbiased, third-party assessment and validation – ensuring inter-institutional comparison. This step supports broader scalability and dissemination of the innovation as it is a peer-referenced outcome. Finally, at the top of the quality assurance Continuum of Excellence, *Institutional Change* happens as the implementation of the innovation is embedded in the institution's strategic plan, policies, practices, incentive structures, budgets, etc. It becomes "hard-wired" as the operational norm.

This model has been applied in practice by Quality Matters (QM). Providing research-supported standards for the design of online courses and programs since 2004, QM has been able to create a widely shared understanding of online course quality with abundant supporting research, validated by application and practice. The Continuum of Excellence in Quality Assurance model was developed from observation of this work as applied in the QM context based on the efforts of approximately 1100 academic institutions in applying the QM Standards to their eLearning initiatives. This model has been shared though conference presentations and focus-group data collected at events and through targeted interviews. Research on this model is continuing, revealing key barriers in moving the innovation of online learning from an ad hoc implementation to standard operating procedure.

EDUCATION TO ALL CORNERS OF THE COUNTRY!

May Tove Dalbakk, Tynset Studie- og høgskolesenter, Norway

Vision of Norwegian Education Centers Association

> *"Our vision is to give the whole country's population the same opportunity to get education regardless of residence, life situation and economy."*

Regional and local education centres are our members.

An education centre is a *generator* in local and regional competence development having knowledge of local business life, knowledge of educational opportunities and providing and facilitating study programmes.

Goals of Norwegian Education Centres Association

- Contribute to cooperation and networking, locally, regionally and nationally;
- Increase the amount of flexible study programs;
- Be a consultative body of flexible education;
- Improve the framework of local education centres;
- Become part of the ordinary Norwegian education system;
- Develop a common standard of quality.

What do the educational centres offer?

- Higher education (university/university college);
- Vocational and higher vocational education;
- Secondary education;
- Formal and informal courses;
- Competency mapping;
- Career guidance and consulting;
- Incorporation and approval of education;
- Practical guidance and follow-up of students;
- Recruitment adapted to local and regional needs.

Benefits for students

- Local opportunities; education along with work, family and leisure;
- No need of travelling;
- Inspiration and motivation by educational peers;
- Participation in learning environment;
- Local exams and lower study expenses.

Benefits for local, regional and central authorities having education centres all over the country

- A national distribution network;
- Lifelong learning to the whole population;
- Cost -effective lifelong learning;
- Optimism and attractiveness in all regions of the country;
- Increased digitalization of education;
- Environmentally friendly.

Our conclusion

Local and regional education centres are "a win-win situation for everyone"!

THE CHALLENGES OF LIFELONG EDUCATION IN INFORMATION SOCIETY – TOWARDS A DIGITAL TURN

Anikó Kálmán, Zoltán Szűts, Budapest University of Technology and Economics, Hungary

In an ideal modern society, citizens have the right to access knowledge and thus take part in lifelong education. In this study, the authors present the practical challenges facing the principle of lifelong learning. On one hand, the challenges are related to the obstacles built by the traditional education system and on another hand, to the context of the information society in which the learning process takes place. The authors are committed to presenting – on the basis of international literature – the theoretical guidelines that characterize the current ecosystem of lifelong learning.

It is evident that lifelong education calls out for making teaching to be both learner and learning centred. This is still regarded as a topical issue. Furthermore, it is essential to restore learning and the organic unity of life (either vertical or horizontal). However, it is just a partial objective and it is neither a new claim. The new factor in education policy today is that the modern state guarantees every citizen's right of access to learning. This means that adults also have the right to study during any stage of their life. This means that the inequality inherent in the system – that legitimizes the reproduction of social inequalities as "natural selection" – can be removed.

There is a clear turn towards the transformation of the educational power centres that seems to have been permanent for centuries because of online communication and social media. All the rituals associated with the phenomenon of learning are reinterpreted. Class attendance (linked to space and time), personal consultation (interpersonal communication with an instructor), teacher-disciple relations (significance of the teacher's personality), taking notes (recording knowledge), will be placed on new, digital foundations.

Teaching-learning and lifelong learning have become an inevitable issue of the changed teacher-student relationship (besides the omniscient teacher, the knowledge that can be found on the network), the question of authentic sources and the way of gaining knowledge independent of space and time and educational institutions. The incorporation of digital devices, content and networks into the everyday life have radically changed the mechanism of obtaining information, reading and learning. There is a need for lifelong learning and immediate knowledge acquisition. In the midst of the information society, the nature of knowledge is changing: it becomes practical, multi-media and transdisciplinary.

THE VALUE OF DEVELOPING AND USING MOOCS FOR SOCIAL INCLUSION

Timothy Read, UNED, Spain, Alastair Creelman, Corina Löwe, Linnaeus University, Sweden, Beatriz Sedano, UNED, Spain

According to the UNHCR (http://www.unhcr.org/5b27be547.pdf), in 2017 there were 68.5 million people forcibly displaced worldwide, of which 25.4 million are refugees, 40.0 million are internally displaced people, and 3.1 million are asylum-seekers. This number has been added to by around 44,400 new displacements every day. It is generally accepted in the academic community that MOOCs could help these people to gain some of the basic knowledge, training, and skills, that might be useful for them to achieve social inclusion, employment, and entrance into higher education. However, there are a range of issues that need to be addressed before these courses can be effective in this sense. Researchers in the MOONLITE project (Massive Open Online courses eNhancing Linguistic and Transversal skills for social inclusion and Employability; ref. no.: 20161ES01KA203025731; http://moonliteproject.eu) have been working on these issues for the past few years and some of the results obtained will be discussed in this workshop so that participants who want to use open education, in the form of MOOCs, for social inclusion can get an understanding of the difficulties that need to be overcome and the types of results that can be expected. Different aspects of this educational process will be presented and analysed in this workshop. It will also be of interest to anyone who wants to develop or use MOOCs in a more inclusive way in general. The starting point are migrants and refugees, but concepts and practices apply to inclusive approaches in general, i.e., how MOOCs can be designed and applied for a broader audience, thereby contributing to an inclusive higher education system.

The issues covered in the workshop include: the problems that refugees have and how MOOCs can be used to help them; the disparity in the perceived value of MOOCs between universities in different European countries; how MOOCs are developed, deployed and run for this group; the problem of the recognition of the learning undertaken in MOOCs and how certification can be undertaken and credits can be awarded; how to overcome the learning styles of refugees and migrants, that may follow an oral tradition, with resistance to open social learning, and with the presence of language difficulties; how mobile learning can be used for the deployment of these courses, even in circumstances where low intermittent network connections are the only ones available; and the best practices that can be applied when considering MOOCs for inclusive formation. The workshop will combine face-to-face interaction and activities with online ones connecting people at the conference with others via the use of synchronous and asynchronous educational technology, collaborative tools, and social networks. Break out groups will be formed to analyse and discuss different aspects of the results of the MOONLITE project that will be presented and discussed in the workshop. All presentations, recorded online interactions, group discussions and analyses will be linked to a Padlet page so that they are available to conference delegate once the event is over. Such a measure will enable discussion and collaboration to continue after the conference finishes. In addition, participants will be invited to join the project's Facebook group, MOOCs for social inclusion and employability (https://www.facebook.com/groups/1836694569953327).

FROM RECIPES IN "HELL'S KITCHEN" TO SERVING IN THE "FIRST DATES RESTAURANT": HOW MIGHT TEACHERS, RATHER THAN DESIGNERS, IN DISTANCE EDUCATION USE ADVANCED LEARNING ANALYTICS?

Tom Olney, The Open University, United Kingdom

This workshop follows on from, "From Beans on Toast to Molecular Gastronomy (and a Bit of MasterChef): Linking Learning Design with Learning Analytics", delivered at EDEN in 2014, and "From Heston back to Jamie: designing an appetising recipe with an ever-changing array of ingredients (designing learning for a world in flux)", delivered to EDEN in 2016. In these workshops we shared how learning analytics and a student focused approach to learning design were being implemented at the Open University (OU) using a celebrity chef metaphor.

Since then, work has continued at the OU to further develop a better understanding of how learning analytics can be combined, visualised and used by teachers in a distance education setting to support students during their studies. Therefore, in 2019 we turn our attention from learning design to teaching practice, or, (in keeping with the extended celebrity food metaphor) from developing recipes in Hell's Kitchen to serving meals in the First Dates Restaurant, in order to share our experiences and findings of these developments.

The workshop will demonstrate how different learning analytics visualisations – specifically including learning design analytics, VLE behaviour and predictive learning analytics – have been piloted by teachers in the Faculty of Science, Technology, Engineering and Mathematics at the OU (STEM-OU) in online learning networks and via dashboards.

Workshop participants will be invited to critically explore a number of these real life representations and discuss how teachers might use them as the basis for action or intervention and to what extent they might be relevant to their own settings. Equally, the question of the challenges and limitations of using learning analytics in this way will be approached. The session will close with a discussion of the findings from the STEM-OU pilot schemes.

AUGMENTED AND VIRTUAL REALITY – IN REALITY CONNECTIONS TO LEARNING, THE WORKPLACE, AND COMMUNITY

Susan C. Aldridge, Drexel University Online, United States of America, Diana Andone, University of Timisoara, Romania, Marci M. Powell, Marci Powell & Associates, United States of America, Steve Wheeler, Plymouth Institution of Education, United Kingdom

Bridging Connections

Augmented and Virtual Reality (AVR) are bridging connections in learning to the workplace and community in ways previously unimaginable, giving rise to an ever-expanding international market. In the last five years, the VR user community has grown from less than one million to 150+ million, and in 2018, the VR market reported staggering profits – $54 billion (47 billion Euro) – from devices alone, while revenue from AR mobile apps topped $725.4 million (633 million Euro) worldwide (Sagar, 2019). Not surprisingly then, academic institutions and business are joining forces around AVR technologies, paving the way for powerful education to workplace connections and applications.

Applications in Business and Education

In fact, industries of all types – from healthcare, manufacturing and retail; to aeronautics, tourism and construction – are exploiting AVR's potential in a variety of innovative ways. Spatial created AR tools for the boardroom and office, enabling its employees to access virtual whiteboards and pin boards, as well as collaboratively work on design documents overlaid on real-world objects (www.zdnet.com/article/augmented-reality-invades-the-conference-room). Walmart is using 17,000 Oculus Go headsets to train its employees in skills ranging from compliance to customer service. Likewise, WayRay, is projecting AR data directly onto a car's windshield, giving navigation prompts, right-of-way information, lane identification and hazard detection (Marr, 2019).

AVR also empowers any number of safely immersive virtual learning environments that feel and respond much as they would in real life, as students engage and explore, interact with and manipulate objects within these worlds. What's more, using sophisticated controls, they can actually "practice" complex procedures like cardiac surgery, or master difficult concepts, such as the molecular properties of brain cells. Some examples include:

- The University of Hamburg developed a VR game called "Therapy for Neurological Diseases".
- Apps like "Anatomyou" make it possible for advanced students to take a non-invasive tour through the body to learn more about its various systems, while "InMind" facilitates a gamified journey through the human brain and "The Body VR" traverses the bloodstream.
- Politehnica University of Timisoara (Romania) and Bentley University (USA) launched the TalkTech Project,(www.talktechproject.net) where students learn to use different technologies to communicate, work, and jointly develop multimedia AVR artifacts (Frydenberg, 2017; Andone & Frydenberg, 2019).
- Drexel University (USA) created VRtifiacts+, a virtual reality repository with more than half a million 360-degree panoramas, simulations and VR, 3D learning objects, which can be incorporated into a course; used to live-stream events, guest lectures and campus tours; or host virtual community spaces.

WHAT DIGITAL COMPETENCES TEACHERS IN HE NEED TODAY?

Sandra Kucina Softic, University Computing Centre University of Zagreb, Croatia

Today we talk and think what digital competences students need to have to be employable when they finish their studies, but in order to ensure that, their teachers need to have digital competences to be able to conduct such teaching and learning. What is digital competence? The European Commission defines digital competence as the confident, critical and creative use of ICT to achieve goals related to work, employability, learning, leisure, inclusion and/or participation in society (Ferrari, 2012). Following Digital Competence Frameworks, Digital Competence Framework for Citizens, Digital Competence Framework for Higher Education institutions and others, in 2018 European Commission released Digital Competence Framework for Educators aiming to help them distinguish digital competences and levels of acquisition. This framework provides a conceptual model, enabling overall, complete and shared understanding of digital competences needed today for efficient and effective teaching and learning.

According to the European Commission's document Open Innovative Teaching and Learning Education through New Technologies and Open Educational Resources (2014), 70% of teachers in the European Union recognize that digital technologies are important for education but only 20-25% of them apply them in teaching. Most teachers use ICT for preparation of teaching and less to work with students and for new ways of teaching. As the reason it is stated that they lack the necessary pedagogical competences for the use of ICT in teaching. It is also stated that 70% of teachers in the European Union want to advance in their profession on ICT skills.

With the advancement of the digital age, teaching methods are being changed, but still it dominantly remains upon teachers to decide whether or not they will follow new technologies and implement them in their teaching. How digital competencies differ from non-digital and can they be separated at all? What digital competences teachers need to have innovative, engaging teaching and active students who will be motivated reach defined learning outcomes? All this will be discussed in this training session. With an introductory topic, the participants will discuss what is the digital competence for them, what are their needs and define what they need to improve the quality of teaching and make it more innovative.

UTILISING A META-DATA STANDARD FOR DIGITAL CREDENTIALS AND RECOGNITION OF OPEN LEARNING

Jochen Ehrenreich, Raimund Hudak, DHBW Duale Hochschule Baden-Württemberg, Germany

Creating Trust and Transparency for Recognizing or Validating Open Learning as ECTS Credits

This workshop will present an extended meta-data standard and a corresponding learning passport for digital credentials and micro-credentials. It will explore possible scenarios, stakeholders and guidelines. The proposed standard adds specific Higher Education and micro-credential extensions to the ESCO metadata schema (European Skills, Competences, Qualifications & Occupations). The aim is to showcase how a secure digital, blockchain-enabled credentialing solution could look like and function, creating a reference for further developments and standardizations. See the full meta-data standard at https://github.com/MicroCredentials/MicroHE.

In order to make an informed and consistent decision on recognizing open learning as ECTS credits towards a degree programme, Higher Education Institutions (HEIs) need sufficient information about a credential. Online education providers on portals such as iversity, edX, Coursera, Udacity, FUN, MiriadaX or XuetangX already provide in-demand skills to the labour market, but to contribute their offerings in the higher education sector as equals to accredited coursed/modules, they need to know which information they should provide and which formal requirements exist regarding workload, learning outcomes, assessment, ID verification, EQF level, quality of learning etc. to make their credentials recognizable. Virtual mobility is also subjected to lack of trust and transpareny, making it difficult to transfer credits from online and other non-traditional short learning programmes:

- which might be offered not only by HEIs, but also by institutions from other education and training sectors;
- which are typically not higher education accredited;
- which are often not described in ECTS, instead use alternative systems of credentials;
- where identity verification and assessment are more complex and challenging than in face-to-face settings;
- without learning agreement or statement from home HEI about the perception of externally acquired learning;
- which lack transparency regarding academic content and learning methodologies.

The recognition and transfer of individual credits through ECTS was created for an era of physical mobility, and is optimised accordingly. Many open education providers are creating parallel systems of credentials - leading to a situation where millions of students per year are enrolling in open courses offered by universities which do not necessarily award valid or recognised forms of credit. Recent studies have tried to provide guidance on the recognition of online learning (Kiron Open Higher Education, 2017; PARADIGMS, 2018; Rampelt, Niedermeier, Röwert, Wallor, & Berthold, 2018; Witthaus et al., 2016) of foreign degrees (The EAR HEI and STREAM projects, 2016) and on secure digital credentialing (Chakroun & Keevy, 2018; Grech & Camilleri, 2017; ICDE, 2019).

A harmonised European approach to recognizing and transferring open education credentials will enable virtual student mobility, empowering students to adapt their learning portfolio to changing labour market demands and new technological trends. Over 60% of children today will work in jobs that currently do not exist (Ibec, 2015). We envisage students becoming digital pioneers and entrepreneurs of their studies as they work on challenging projects and seek out learning resources online or from other specialist sources (Code University of Applied Sciences, 2019). We envisage HEIs adapting their curricula and accompanying their students on their open learning journey.

OEPass: Open Education Passport – Improving the Portability and Recognition of Open Learning, https://oepass.eu/

MicroHE: Supporting Learning Excellence through Micro-Credentialing in Higher Education,
https://microcredentials.eu/

PREPARING DISTANCE LEARNERS FOR LIVING IN THE WORLD – A MANIFESTO FOR THE DEVELOPMENT OF INFORMATION LITERACY / CRITICAL INFORMATION FLUENCY

Sandra Tury, David Baume, University of London, United Kingdom

This workshop explores the current state of play of critical information literacy in the context of distance education. It identifies what distance learning educators and information professionals are currently doing, and what more they can and should do, to ensure that students develop and demonstrate the necessary sophisticated information capabilities. It is based on a research project located at the University of London's Centre for Distance Education (CDE). The aim of the study is to equip all University of London's distance learning students (50,000 from180 countries) with Critical Information Literacy (CIL) skills not only to complete their programmes successfully, but also to go on to work independently, efficiently and competently in an open and connected world. This will in turn open up the world of education to wider and more diverse participants.

Technology now enables us to connect with and use much of the world's information. Doing this is (a) a vital life and work skill and (b) difficult. Doing this well requires what we term critical information fluency (CIF). This describes a set of abilities, dispositions, and indeed compulsions. The definition of this term is still a work in progress but a current version suggests: "I am critically information fluent when, as a matter of course, I: (a) identify what information I need; (b) identify why (and perhaps also when) I need it; (c) find it efficiently; (d) evaluate it rigorously according to explicit and appropriate criteria; (e) use / process it for my intended academic / professional purpose(s); (f) communicate it clearly, accurately, in ways that are both appropriate to the intended audience(s) and ethical; (g) give sound reasons for my decisions and actions at each stage."

This emergent account of critical information fluency builds on, and goes a beyond, the valuable account of information literacy (IL) as: "Knowing when and why you need information, where to find it, and how to evaluate, use and communicate it in an ethical manner" (CILIP, 2004). It promotes a more active form that focuses on doing rather than knowing. Interim conclusions from the study suggest that:

- As a sector, higher education is under-ambitious about the kinds of information literacies and fluencies which our graduates need now, let alone for the future.
- We see signs of more ambitious work on information literacy / critical information fluency in project modules, and also in postgraduate study.
- The UoL Online Library has pioneered and so far has integrated IL into 6 different PG programmes with remarkable results in terms of increased library use, enquiry complexity, quality of dissertations, attainment, etc. These findings were the motivation for the CDE project.
- However, information literacy / fluency is much bigger than just a library issue. Indeed. IL is specified in the requirements of accrediting bodies. Being information literate in a good and supportive library is about as big an achievement as not starving in a supermarket. It is useful, but nothing like enough.
- Information literacy / critical information fluency need to be embedded in curriculum, in pedagogy, and also of course in assessment, and in discipline-appropriate forms. This requires close collaboration between library and library-supporting faculty.
- Without an institutional policy and strategy that makes Information literacy / critical information fluency a requirement, current fragmented local initiatives by enthusiasts are unlikely to come together to achieve the necessary synergies.

There is a dilemma. We want to be helpful to our students, and so we typically give them ready access, including via hyperlinks, to some, most or even all of the required reading for their course. We teach them any skills that are currently necessary to use the databases. We make accessing the specified sources as easy as we can. (This may be a particularly severe issue in distance education, where we cannot make the same assumptions about access to a physical library as we can with institution-based students.) And so we simultaneously enable them in the very short term, and fail to enable them for the longer term.

GOODBYE ADMINISTRATION HASSLE, HELLO FEEDBACK!

Johan van den Heuvel, Kerim Haccou, Ans Exam BV, the Netherlands

Introduction

Today, a lot is going digital in the education world. All the course material can be found online, many assignments are submitted digitally and a large part of the tests is taken digitally. The benefits are clear and time saving is a big gain for the teacher. But what does the student actually think of this new trend? Is he or she actually as satisfied with digital testing as the teacher? And are there perhaps other alternatives to save time? Two former students are presenting their solution for getting rid of administration hassle and providing better feedback.

Quality perceived by students

As students, Kerim and Johan, experienced that there is not that much feedback provided to the students after they finished an exam. It is hard to review your own exam. Professors don't have enough time to talk with every student about their exams and results. Moreover, professors don't have enough time for doing the grading as well and they sometimes have to "force" their exams into a multiple-choice exam. Since we are both from an engineering university, this was a big quality drop of the exams. With engineering, we were used to work with a lot of formulas and drawings in order to come up with a final answer. Previously, the process was the most important, today the final answer is key!

Solution – Ans Delft

Many students shared these experiences with us, therefore it was time for change! What if the digital world could be combined with the paper world? Could we provide the freedom of paper with the administration benefits of the digital environment? That's where Ans Delft started. A platform in which most of the exam process is digital, but where the students still have the freedom of paper. We have a solution for scanning paper exams and grading them online. This system is used by more than 2000 professors in The Netherlands and Belgium today. Besides that, we also have a user-friendly digital exam tool.

Benefits

With Ans it is possible to save a lot of time in the whole exam process, but it also offers some benefits to the students. After the professors finished their grading, they can publish their results. This means that a student can finds his results online and is able to ask questions about this via the tool. If you want to get a better understanding of the platform, please visit our workshop or send us a message!

INNOVATING INTERNATIONAL HIGHER EDUCATION BY VIRTUAL MOBILITY

George Ubachs, EADTU, the Netherlands

Blended and virtual mobility is stimulated in many Erasmus+ actions, in particular in the "European universities" initiative, "strategic partnerships", "knowledge alliances", "sector skills" and "capacity building". The "eU.University hub" for online learning will stimulate and empower universities for online education and virtual mobility. In the Erasmus+ 2019 call, virtual mobility is defined as "a set of activities supported by Information and Communication Technologies, including e-learning, that realise or facilitate international, collaborative experiences in a context of teaching, training or learning". In this workshop on VM we bring together stakeholders to reflect on the opportunities offered by virtual mobility by reflecting on:

How virtual mobility can stimulate European universities:

- exploring the potential of VM within European universities and university networks;
- generating (political) support for VM becoming a mainstream mobility scheme.

Good practices of virtual mobility;

- overview of current good practices concerning virtual mobility;
- overview of cooperation models for virtual exchange programmes.

New developments in the field of virtual mobility:

- sharing of current institutional and curriculum-level plans by the participants for the development of VM;
- Identifying opportunities and obstacles in VM at institutional and student level.

Part of this are interactive WG sessions in which we discuss in groups the state of affairs of VM in Europe so far and how VM could be further developed within institutional, national and European frameworks. We aim to create 3 groups and bring results to the table at the end of the workshop.

EXPLORING A FRAMEWORK FOR SHAPING TOMORROW, TACKLING EMERGING CHALLENGES TODAY

Paula Shaw, University of Derby, United Kingdom

Visualising an Online Ecosystem; Creating the PROPHET Framework

Recognising the opportunities that online education could offer, the University of Derby decided to take the radical step to remove fully online education from faculties and create a specialist department dedicated to these students and University of Derby Online Learning (UDOL) was born. The department was tasked with creating an institutional framework for delivering online learning, an ecosystem to remove technology from its central position in distance education and replaced it with learner-centred educational values. Horizon scanning is at the centre of the framework's future-focused thinking; enabling the addition and removal of conceptual pedagogies and learning technologies. As the framework has evolved it has been given an acronym title to accurately represent its function, the now named PROPHET framework recognises the importance of creating a yin-yang balance between Pedagogic Realignment, Organisational Priorities and Horizon Emergent Technologies.

Evolving the Framework Through Design-Based Research and Conceptual Analysis

A Design-based longitudinal approach was adopted to continually refine this framework. Not a methodology itself, Design-based research draws on a variety of traditional methods to achieve its goal. For this framework, design-based research provides the lifecycle and iterative refresh that is needed for the conceptual analysis of cutting-edge technology enhanced learning in real-world environments. Conceptual Analysis (CA) is used by academics to work with abstract ideas to deliver empirical results. In simple linguistic terms it means thinking, discussing, defining and agreeing on common truths. However, in practice this over simplification denigrates the time it takes to arrive at a common understanding. Exploring Conceptual Analysis has been described as a semantic puzzle and a paradox of analysis; solving a semantic conundrum opens the opportunity for substantive discovery, by uncovering fine-grained differences in meaning allows us to differentiate between statements (Balcerak Jackson, 2013). Taking the example of *online learning* itself, there is a recognition that *online* means *via the internet*, and *learning* means acquired knowledge, from this perspective any acquired knowledge gained from the internet would satisfy this definition. Thus, people use this term interchangeably from low-level informal internet learning, to formal study with internet-delivered content. The online arena is further compounded by new innovations, making it difficult to pin-down long-term definitions.

How Can We Tackle Emerging Challenges On the Horizon, Today?

This workshop introduces strategic planners and practitioners to the PROPHET framework, using it to investigate organisational practices through Conceptual Analysis and take control of their educational needs. Through this highly interactive workshop, participants will consider their institutions infrastructure then explore a Horizon Challenge; collaboratively producing a refined version of the framework to address their own specific pedagogic and educational planning needs. Having actively worked through the framework participants will be equipped with a tool that is ready to be applied to emerging trends and challenges within their own institution. The workshop uses a coaching method based on "The Coaching Habit" (Stanier, 2016) to encourage participation in the activities, asking participants to explore "what is on their mind?" and "What is the real challenge for them" will encourage personal reflection throughout.

Using a coaching method participants will explore challenges that will have a disruptive effect on Higher Education.

SUSTAINABLE CONFERENCES AND PROJECTS – TIME FOR VIRTUAL COLLABORATION

Alastair Creelman, Linnaeus University, Niklas Brinkfeldt, Dalarna University, Sweden

We have all benefited greatly in our professional lives from the ability to travel freely around the world. Through international conferences and projects, we have all built professional networks that have been invaluable to our development. By participating in meetings, conferences and projects, we have formed valuable partnerships that have resulted in research, course development, new career paths and new projects. It is hard to imagine what our careers would have looked like without these inspiring contacts, thanks to the easy access to international travel.

Today, however, we see all too clearly the effects of growing levels of carbon emissions and the resulting effects on our climate. It is therefore essential that we all try to reduce our carbon footprint and one way to do this is to reduce the amount of air travel we undertake. Many of us in education are involved in projects, conferences and exchange programmes that all demand frequent air travel and as a result, our activities have a high carbon footprint. As professionals in the field of distance and e-learning, it is surely time for us to fully exploit digital platforms and tools to reduce our need to travel. In this workshop, we will investigate alternative forms of international collaboration and see if we can find a more sustainable platform for our activities. Of course, physical meetings are vital for networking, building trust and establishing partnerships but if such meetings are to become rarer, in the future we need to find alternatives that provide the best possible opportunities for international cooperation.

Many conferences offer streamed keynote talks, often with very professional video quality, but streaming workshop sessions presents many challenges if the online participants are to feel included in the session instead of simply being passive observers. Technologies such as the use of 360-degree cameras and 3D can give the online participants the ability to look around the room and get a sense of presence and collaborative online tools can facilitate real time interaction between online and on-site participants. However, it often proves difficult for organisers to charge fees for such online participation and guarantee value for money.

Already there are many examples of virtual conferences, such as the Sakai virtual conference, and programmes of open online seminars such as Open Education Week. EDEN is involved in several such initiatives and they attract many participants. In addition, virtual mobility activities are gaining ground in many countries, notably with the launching of the Erasmus+ virtual exchange programme and several innovative international projects. Online conferences often focus on content delivery and even if today's platforms offer scope for increasingly collaborative webinars there are some important aspects of the on-site conference that are hard to replicate in online spaces.

One of the main reasons for attending an on-site conference is to build professional networks and the opportunity for chance meetings in the coffee or lunch queue or at an evening mingle session. Similarly, the transition time between sessions offers an opportunity to greet colleagues or exchange a few comments with a new acquaintance. These conversations are a way to process impressions and new insights from the conference sessions. Online conferences need to be able to offer spaces for such interaction, the digital equivalents of a coffee queue, a lounge area, a garden or an informal reception. Another challenge commonly expressed by participants of online conferences is the difficulty of devoting time to the conference while sitting in the office where everyday duties inevitably take priority. Travelling to a conference is for many academics an opportunity to step outside the everyday bubble and focus on competence development and networking. Staying in the office makes this escape almost impossible. Many people sign up for online conferences and webinars but are unable to attend or focus on the activity because their main duties will always have higher priority.

In this workshop, we will discuss how we can develop hybrid conferences, collaboration spaces and facilitate the invaluable informal meetings and networking that takes place in on-site conferences, especially during breaks and meal times. This workshop will present an outline of these themes as well as presenting some examples of good practice.

POP-UP CLASSROOM: CREATING POSSIBILITIES AND INSPIRATION FOR THE INTEGRATION OF NEW TECHNOLOGIES IN HIGHER EDUCATION LEARNING ENVIRONMENTS

Sylke Vandercruysse, Stefanie Dujardin, Kurt Galle, VIVES University of Applied Sciences, Belgium

The vision and ambition of VIVES in the field of education is formulated in an education policy plan. The main goal is to prepare its students for tomorrow's professions by developing student-centred learning environments in which students become active, self-managing and cooperative learners. The most recent education policy plan focusses on different topics in order to work on this general goal, such as intensifying the collaboration with workplaces, stimulating interdisciplinarity, retain an effective teaching-research nexus, developing digital competence and obtaining educational goals by educational technology.

Every year, the spotlights are put on one aspect of the education policy plan. In the academic year of 2018-2019, the spotlight will be put on "educational technology". Technology and digitization will undoubtedly be decisive in shaping future-proof training. It is crucial to monitor these technological evolutions and developments and to estimate to what extent these evolutions and developments should be included in the study programs (Beckers et al., 2018). With the annual theme "Driven by Technology" an attempt is made to give everyone in VIVES the necessary drive to discover the possibilities of technology, to use them in a well thought-out way and to make courses future-proof.

Preparing students for work in a rapidly changing, digitized context can only be effective if the learning context is also technology-rich. Technology can give our education an extra dimension and strengthen it if we are able to implement it thoughtfully in our daily activities. Hence, preparing for a digital workplace requires that the teacher also possesses technological competences (Sels, Vansteenkiste, & Knipprath, 2017). The education policy plan attaches importance to this through the sub-goal: "Every teacher has the necessary digital competences to use educational technology in a goal-oriented way". Therefore, in addition to the abovementioned efforts, a blended learning approach is stimulated and professionalization initiatives are set up in order to stimulate well designed technology-rich learning environments.

Professionalization is necessary because it forms an important lever in the awareness process about the importance and the added value of educational technology. If this belief is not present, teachers are more inclined to commit adhere to routines (Tondeur, Valcke, & Braak, 2008; Voogt, Fisser, & Tondeur 2010). Organizing professionalization activities can also help to stimulate digital competencies among teachers and raise awareness of their importance.

In the context of the annual theme, it was decided to create a pop-up classroom in academic year 2018-2019. The purpose of this pop-up classroom is twofold. On the one hand, we want to bring the new range of technologies and applications to the teachers. Teachers get the chance to see what technological novelties are available and how they can use them during their lessons or for their education. On the other hand, VIVES also wants to inspire teachers in the pop-up classroom: what does the future bring? And do teachers like this? What do they want to try and do they have ideas about new technologies or applications that they would like to try – with the necessary support? Hence, in this classroom we want to trigger our teachers with new and existing technologies with new features. We want to stimulate them to think how technology can enhance and enrich their learning environment.

The design of the pop-up classroom had to be flexible, creative and innovative. The pop-up classroom consists of 5 zones:

- virtual and collaboration room (red);
- educational technology zone (orange);
- artificial intelligence zone (yellow);
- virtual / augmented / mixed reality zone (green);
- brainstorm zone (blue).

During this demo-session, the different zones are explained and in each zone, a selection of tools or applications are highlighted.

EVALUATION IN DISTANCE EDUCATION @ VIVES: SOME TOOLS AND TRENDS

Hendrik Coucke, Koen Verhulst, Sylke Vandercruysse, VIVES University of Applied Sciences, Belgium

Preparing students for work in a rapidly changing, digitised context can only be done effectively if the learning context is also technology rich (Sels, Vansteenkiste, & Knipprath, 2017). For this purpose, teachers – as engineers and designers of their own learning environment – must have the necessary expertise to present subject-specific knowledge and skills to students in an attractive and comprehensible way using technology. This triple expertise is clearly described in the TPACK model: when content knowledge, didactic knowledge and technological knowledge are integrated, they can reinforce each other and offer an excellent basis for a lesson in which technology is integrated in a meaningful way (Koehler & Mishra, 2009).

The effectiveness of blended learning is influenced by whether or not digital evaluation is used. Digital evaluation means that you use technology and ICT to develop, assemble, administer, assess and / or analyse assessment instruments. It is known that online testing, self-testing and quizzes can lead to more effective learning in different ways: through the testing effect, through the spread effect and through the effect of feedback (Spanjers, Könings, Leppink, & van Merriënboer, 2014).

In comparison with analogue testing, there are - in addition to the learning effect - some benefits associated with digital evaluation. For instance, multimedia can be added, such as videos, hyperlinks, interactive images, etc. and is more in line with the blended approach to educational practices (Kennisnet, 2017). Using digital tests or exams can reduce paper and correction time and also the organisation of exams can be optimised. Moreover, it also offers opportunities for a more personal and customised approach: the assessment can be more flexible (i.e., location and time independent) and the tests can be better tailored to the individual progress of the student; testing can be made adaptive, so that differentiation in the assessment itself is possible. Teachers can also work with a pool of questions by creating an item database together with colleagues. This allows a teacher to bring variety to the tests. Digital assessment tools often offer the opportunity to collect data about the learning process and also information about the performance level of the (individual) students can be more easily generated. Of course there are also a number of disadvantages associated with digital assessment. These disadvantages arise especially when the teachers, students or the ICT infrastructure of the school are not sufficiently equipped to perform digital testing. It is therefore important to devote enough time and energy to the preparation of digital assessment.

In order to use digital testing in a qualitative way, the use of good and appropriate tools is crucial. VIVES has therefore – especially with a view to distance learning courses – invested in the development of new tools to facilitate digital assessment. During this demo a number of these tools are explained:

- *The exam centre* offers the possibility to take exams with a lot of students at the same time. By bringing students from all distance training courses together at a moment that fits best for the students, a higher degree of flexibility is obtained.
- *ProctorExam* is used for the organisation of the remote examinations because in VIVES, students from distance education programs can take examinations remotely.
- *AssessmentQ/Edumatic* is an online environment for offering digital exercises and taking online exams. The teacher has the possibility to create an exercise database in which he/she can choose from about 20 different question types.

Synergy

ABC to VLE

ABC to VLE beyond curriculum design

Website: https://abc-ld.org/abc-to-vle/

Runtime: 09/2018– 08/2020

Supported / co-funded by: Erasmus+ Key Action 203

Partners: ABC to VLE Coordinator, University College London (UCL), UK, see more at https://abc-ld.org/abc-to-vle/abc-to-vle-partners/.

Project representative to be contacted for further info: Nataša Perović (n.perovic@ucl.ac.uk)

ABC to VLE is a 2 year Erasmus+ funded collaborative project, including 12 partner European institutions, and lead by University College London (UCL). Europe. The project is developing support toolkits to help course teams to implement their ABC learning designs within the local Virtual Learning Environment (VLE) or Learning Management System (LMS).

ABC LD (Young and Perović, 2016) is a rapid course design method, derived from the conversational framework theory by Professor Diana Laurillard (Laurillard, 2012). This method is now being used in many universities across Europe and has gained significant interest from academics and course designers. The project will further develop the ABC toolkit to enable universities to localise the method for their own strategic, pedagogical and technical context, with a focus on the functionality and potential of the institutional VLE/LMS.

In this synergy session, project partner institutions will discuss their localised applications of the ABC method and report on their findings. These local applications will include, among others, using the ABC method for academic development, designing MOOCs with the ABC, empowering students by including them in the course design process, etc. Participants in this symposium will appreciate some of the more advanced applications of the ABC method and will be able to reflect and discuss the applicability of it within their own educational contexts.

The following partner universities intend to participate:

University College London (UCL), University of Milan, University of Helsinki, University of Zagreb, Sorbonne University, University Polytechnic Timisoara, VIVES university of applied sciences.

Main target groups of the project: Higher education, teachers, educators, academic developers, course designers.

Significant public results: https://abc-ld.org/abc-to-vle

Europeana Media

Europeana Media

Universal Media europeana Player

Website: https://pro.europeana.eu/project/europeana-media

Runtime: 09.2018 – 03.2020

Supported / co-funded by: Innovation and Networks Executive Agency / Department C - Connecting Europe Facility (CEF) - TELECOMMUNICATIONS SECTOR

Partners: Istituto Luce Cinecittà, Italy; Netherlands Institute for Sound and Vision, The Netherlands; Europeana Foundation, The Netherlands; Noterik B.V., The Netherlands; Technische Informationsbibliothek, Germany; Audiovisual Technologies, Informatics and Telecommunications, Belgium

Project representative to be contacted for further info: Sally REYNOLDS (sally.reynolds@atit.be)

Europeana Media aims to develop an Enhanced Unified Playout Service (EUPS), offering heritage institutions a media playout with market-competitive quality, user friendly design, and cross-border content reusability.

It will increase the appeal, visibility, reuse, research and interaction with Europe's AV heritage available directly through Europeana Collections and third-party platforms that use Europeana content, especially for users in education (at all levels) and research.

Europeana Collections has shortcomings in user experience related to video content and audio recordings that prevent AV material from reaching its full potential:

1. differing playout services used by content providers;
2. current playout on Europeana offers no additional features that make AV more appealing and reusable;
3. AV content reuse is often hindered by not providing clear information related to reuse.

Europeana Media addresses these shortcomings through the development of the EUPS. In particular, it will deliver functionalities that will offer researchers, educators and citizens to better access and incorporate AV content from Europeana into their working environments, such as video fragment quoting, support for subtitling, and embedding media. In addition, the EUPS will be integrated into the Europeana Core platform, ensuring long-term sustainability.

In order to ensure that the EUPS fully meets the needs and requirements of the key target users in education and research, the project follows the user-centred design approach (DIN EN ISO 9241-210). For the needs analysis we conducted interviews with six researchers, nine educators, and two generic users that used videos found in online video repositories for varying needs. The results of the survey show common patterns of use of online media by the majority of educators and researchers. The need for personal annotations to full videos or segments and subtitle them, the need to export bibliographic metadata from entire videos or segments and embed videos or segments, for example in electronic learning environments such as Moodle, in social media, or in CMSs like WordPress and Drupal. All interviewees expect licence information to be provided to know what they are allowed to do with the videos. Furthermore, the participants expect online video repositories to be reliable by supporting content accessibility, searchability, reusability, and quotability.

Main target groups of the project: teachers and educators, content developers, educational publishers at all levels (Primary, Secondary, Higher and Further Education), researchers

Significant public results: Guidelines and recommendations for the development and use of online video repositories for education and research, improved access to media on Europeana by mans of the EUPS.

eLene4Life

Learning and Interacting to Foster Employability

Website: http://elene4life.eu

Runtime: 09.2018 – 08.2021

Supported / co-funded by: Erasmus+ KA2 Grant Agreement N°: 2018-1-FR01-KA203-047829

Partners: Fondation UNIT – AUNEGe (FR) (Coordinator); Fondazione Politecnico di Milano (IT); Politecnico di Milano (IT); European University College Association (BE); Warsaw University of Technology (PL); Universität Bremen (DE); Liberia Universita Maria SS Assunta di Roma (IT); University of Dundee (UK).

Project representative to be contacted for further info: Deborah Arnold (projets@aunege.fr)

Project description: eLene4Life supports curriculum innovation in higher education (HE) through the development of active learning approaches for soft skills, with the ultimate aim of improving students' employability.

According to the 2018 World Economic Forum Report "Towards a Reskilling Revolution: A Future of Jobs for All", the rise of artificial intelligence, robotics and other digital developments is upending the primacy of human expertise in the economy. The individuals who will succeed in the economy of the future will be those who can complement the work done by mechanical or algorithmic technologies, and "work with the machines". The 2018 European Commission Proposal on Key Competences also draws attention to these disruptions affecting European societies and economies, stating that "Skills such as creativity, critical thinking, taking initiative and problem solving play an important role in coping with complexity and change in today's society".

In a previous Erasmus+ project, eLene4work, the development of HE students' (digital) soft skills was experimented through the use of MOOCs and OERs. The results showed that, while autonomous learning indeed played a significant role, real impact would only come from fully integrating these into the curriculum.

Project goals

- overcome skills mismatches with respect to transversal skills;
- develop new innovative curricula and educational methods integrating active learning, at the same time addressing commonly encountered barriers such as large class sizes and physical spaces;
- improve the relevance of HE curricula in Partner Countries in a VUCA (Volatile, Uncertain, Complex, Ambiguous) world.

Actions and outputs:

Concretely, eLene4life will develop a series of outputs and related activities:

- Two parallel Foresight Analyses will gather examples of active learning approaches in HE (O1) and the corporate sector (O2).
- These will serve as input to a Dynamic Toolkit (O3), implemented and tested in Pilot Projects (O4) in 5 countries (DE, FR, IT, PL, UK).
- O5, a discussion-based MOOC, offers professional development opportunities to the wider community of HE teachers.
- Cross-sectoral collaboration runs throughout the project, supported by a University-Corporate Community of Practice (O6).
- Finally, the lessons learned during the project will be compiled into three attractive publications (O7: LLK) to support decision-making and the wider uptake of active learning for transversal skills development.

Main target groups of the project: HE leaders, teachers, students, alumni; HR managers, trainers, training providers.

Significant public results: published on the eLene4Life hub as they become available throughout the project http://elene4life.eu/project-outputs/

EFE

Entrance into future education

ENTRANCE TO FUTURE EDUCATION

Website: http://www.efe-project.eu

Runtime: 02.2019 – 12.2019

Supported / co-funded by: Erasmus+

Partners: Latvia University, Latvia; UC Leuven-Limburg, Belgium; University of Humanities and Economics in Lodz (AHE), Poland; Media & Learning Association, Belgium.

Project representative to be contacted for further info: Sally Reynolds (sally.reynolds@atit.be)

The aim of the Entrance to Future Education project is to highlight teaching methods that engage, motivate, inspire students and help them to develop the skills required for the 21st century labour market. This project aims this way at contributing to the innovation of academic teaching practice.

The methods have been compiled through our own contributions and research and by interviewing students and academics in focus groups. The result is the development of methodological material called "Student-centred Teaching Methods for the Development of 21st Century Skills".

Main target groups of the project: higher education teaching staff interested in innovating their teaching practice

Significant public results: A manual is the main result of the first year of activities by the partners and provides a resource of 40 methods and approaches that can be applied in a wide variety of European higher education institutions. Both new as well as experienced teaching staff in universities and colleges interested in applying new methods and approaches in their teaching are targeted with this work.

These methods and approaches are being piloted, validated and enhanced by the partners as part of the second year of project activities The examples of the pilots are a part of the manual as well.

LiveLab

The importance of a Team-based Interprofessional Practice Placement (TIPP) in primary care to increase Interprofessional Collaboration (IPC) for undergraduate healthcare students

Website: https://www.vives.be/nl/labs/livelab

Runtime: 09.2018 –09.2022

Supported / co-funded by: VIVES University of Applied Sciences

Partners: VIVES University of Applied Sciences, Community of Houthulst, Blankenberge, Roeselare, Wervik, Beernem, Oostkamp and Gistel.

Project representative to be contacted for further info: Tony Claeys, project coordinator (tony.claeys@vives.be), Lisa Kerckhof, coordinator Centre of Expertise of Care Innovation (lisa.kerckhof@vives.be).

Facing challenges for curricula

As Interprofessional Education (IPE) is often a challenge to organize for healthcare students due to different factors, literature shows crucial aspects to make IPE important for all involved health care students. Implementing interprofessional education in curricula mimicking real life practice can enhance learning and this transfer can be favourable for students to learn and practice. Interprofessional collaboration (IPC) is not only challenging for health care workers but also for health educators who have the responsibility to prepare health care students, thus requiring IPC training in the curricula. It is important to introduce health care students to real-world experiences outside the classroom in a social context of collaborative and experiential learning. Interdisciplinary placements in primary care create some of these real-life opportunities for students to generate interprofessional expertise. Interprofessional placements in primary care for ungraduated healthcare students are sparse and research about this topic is almost non-existent. It provides opportunities for health care students to develop problem-solving abilities from a broader perspective and with a patient-centred perspective. There is little evidence on how we can train IPC with students and real patients in real life settings. In order to train students for IPC within IPE, it is necessary to create training in similar clinical environments whereby students provide patient care similar to what will be expected of them in primary care.

Teamwork during placements in primary care

The goal of IPE for students is to learn how to function in an interprofessional student team; this functioning has been described as interprofessional collaborative practice (ICP). ICP describes the elements of IPC implemented in practice settings similar to placements in primary care and TIPP. Development of teamwork skills is an essential foundation for effective ICP and teaching interprofessional teamwork skills is one of the goals of IPE an essential component of effective IPC. Evidence on how this ICP as TIPP should be organized in primary care is not fully studied. During TIPP students should learn how to function in an interprofessional team and many of the competencies proposed for IPE are related to teamwork. Placements for healthcare students in primary care can train these teamwork skills. Real-world experiences in primary health care offer a unique learning environment for health care students to practice interprofessional patient-centred clinical practice. Health care simulation has shown to improve students' attitudes toward IPC and teamwork communication skills, but research on how IPE relates to IPC during placements in primary care remains undiscovered. Students need opportunities to acquire teamwork skills suitable for IPC within a patient care context. Patients can contribute to healthcare education in different ways. At high level patients can help to design learning and reviewing educational interventions. Educators have facilitating roles during IPE and find it very challenging to interact with interprofessional student teams. Literature shows improved teamwork skills in simulated settings but IPC in primary care settings remains undiscovered. The crucial aspects of effective interprofessional teamwork in primary care settings are obscure and there is an urgent need to investigate these crucial elements of effective teamwork. One way we can observe these elements of ICP is during interprofessional placements in primary care. Only a few number of studies have observed this data to explore the complex phenomena of interprofessional teamwork in primary care settings. In situ training during placements in primary care are recognized of great educational value. The mix of training and observing students in interprofessional teamwork during interprofessional placement in primary care can uncover important aspects for training healthcare students in IPC in future curricula.

Main target groups of the project: primary care, students, teachers, healthcare workers.
Significant public results: no results available.

OEPASS

Open Education Passport

Website: https://oepass.eu/

Runtime: 1 Nov 2017 - 31 Jan 2020

Supported / co-funded by: Erasmus + KA2 Cooperation for Innovation and the Exchange of Good Practices

Partners: Duale Hochschule Baden-Württemberg Heilbronn, Germany; Stifterverband, Germany; EDEN European Distance and E-Learning Network Lbg, United Kingdom; BME Budapesti Műszaki és Gazdaságtudományi Egyetem, Hungary; LieDM Asociacija, Lithuania; Knowledge Innovation Centre Ltd, Malta; UNED Universidad Nacional de Education a Distancia, Spain; TAU Tampere University, Finnland.

Project representatives to be contacted for further info: Jochen Ehrenreich (jochen.ehrenreich@heilbronn.dhbw.de) and Ferenc Tatrai (tatrai@eden-online.org)

The project aims at creating a solution to make online and open learning comparable and recognisable within higher education. It will optimise the recognition of individual credits with respect to opportunities and structure of open education and virtual mobility.

Establishing a concept of a "quality credential", creating a standard format for describing open education and virtual mobility experiences in terms of ECTs are in the focus of the project through a proposed framework for the automatic exchange of information about open educational experience and its recognition.

The project will significantly expand the European knowledge-base on recognition of open learning through

- A quality system for analysing the quality of credentials through a lens of ease-of-recognition and portability;
- Creating a Learning Passport: a standard form to collect information about open education experiences;
- Recognition and verification of credentials in open education by a proposal for a technological infrastructure to support the portability and recognition of open credentials;
- A methodology for the calculation, verification and assessment of learning outcomes and workload in digital environments using ECTS for open education;
- Realising the scope of Open Education through credentialisation. The report will look at the future of Open Education, by considering a set of scenarios where education is fully open or fully closed, and where the systems of credentialisation is fully open or fully closed.

Main target groups of the project: students, employers, universities and recognition, authorities, teachers and course-designers in open education, policy-and-decision makers.

Significant public results: The project will

- Propose a *concept of quality assurance* whereby credentials would be assessed in terms of their transparency, portability, recognition by employers and academia, stackability and a number of other factors. It will also propose an initial quality-hierarchy for the most-common open education credentials currently being offered.
- Propose a standard format for describing open education and virtual mobility experiences in terms of ECTS called *Learning Passport,* capturing a wide range of non-formal and formal open education experiences. A first draft of the Learning Passport is available at https://oepass.eu/outputs/learningpassport/
- Outline an *ontology for the recognition of open-learning*, together with *a meta-data standard and technology roadmap*, which would allow for the automatic exchange of credit between European Higher Education Institutions.

Skill Up

Matching Graduates' Skills and Labour World Demands through Authentic Learning Scenarios

Website: http://skill-up-project.eu

Runtime: 09.2016 – 06.2019

Supported / co-funded by: Erasmus+ Programme

Partners: Universitat Oberta de Catalunya, Spain (coord.); Stockholm University, Sweden; Technical University of Applied Sciences Wildau, Germany; Institut Obert de Catalunya, Spain; Fundació Factor Humà, Spain; University of Applied Labour Studies, Germany.

Project representative to be contacted for further info: Adriana Ornellas (aornellas@uoc.edu)

The gap between the fast-paced demands for new skills in the European labour markets and the slow pace of the diverse European educational systems to meet these demands persists. At the policy level, the solutions are ambitious: the 2014 "Education and Training Monitor", calls for all learners in all European countries to be equipped with the required skills to successfully participate in society and the labour market. Specifically, the report calls for: (a) strengthening the quality and relevance of Higher Education programmes, focusing on boosting graduates employability; (b) involving employers in the development and quality assurance of programmes as a means for linking more closely the worlds of education and work; (c) combining innovative pedagogies with an effective use of digital tools and content to foster more innovative methods of learning, and far-reaching access to learning resources and learning opportunities.

The project Skill Up aimed to build scalable and replicable ways for connecting higher education curricula with evolving labour market demands. The specific objectives of the project were to:

1. Map good practices in matching graduates' skills and labour market demands through authentic learning scenarios in higher education.
2. Improve soft and hard employability skills of undergraduates by means of designing, developing, applying and evaluating authentic learning scenarios in higher education and vocational education and training settings.
3. Enhance access to lifelong career counselling and guidance (CGC) for undergraduates and graduates by training CGC practitioners by means of a MOOC on "E-guidance in Higher Education to Promote Graduates' Lifelong Career Development".
4. Implement and promote a virtual environment that acts as a hub for attracting stakeholders, offering guidance to labour market newcomers and real hands-on experiences in the professional world as part of students' learning.

Main target groups of the project: Higher Education faculty, Vocational education and training teachers, career counsellors and advisors, undergraduates, graduates and employers.

Significant public results:

- Report Good practices in connecting workplace and learning in higher education. Available at http://skill-up-project.eu/wp-content/uploads/2017/05/IO1_Report_final_English-1.pdfhttp://skill-up-project.eu/wp-content/uploads/2017/05/IO1_Report_final_English-1.pdf
- Infographics summarizing key issues on employability skills and authentic learning environments. Available at http://skill-up-project.eu/wp-content/uploads/2017/05/skill_up_V5.pdf
- Multiplier event Erasmus+ Skill Up Project: Extending the scope: Authentic learning, and Career Counseling and Guidance in Higher Education. Program available at http://skill-up-project.eu/multiplier-events/
- MOOC on E-guidance in Higher Education to Promote Graduates' Lifelong Career Development. Available at https://mooc.skill-up-project.eu/courses/UOCx/001/2019_T1/about
- Authentic scenarios for enhancing new graduates' employability skills on universities and vocational education and training settings. http://skill-up-project.eu/results-ios/io2/
- Skill Up hub. http://skill-up-project.eu/results-ios/io4/

DigiCulture

Improving the Digital Competences and Social Inclusion of Adults in Creative Industries

Website: http://www.digiculture.eu

Runtime: 10.2018 – 03.2021

Supported / co-funded by: Erasmus+ Strategic Partnership

Partners: Politehnica University of Timisoara, Romania; Universita degli Studi Roma Tre, Italy; Aalborg University, Denmark; Graz University, Austria; Dublin City University, Ireland; Timisoara European Capital of Culture Association, Romania; JME Associates, UK; National Association of Distance Education, Lithuania.

Project representative to be contacted for further info: Dr. Diana Andone (diana.andone@upt.ro)

The main outcomes of the DigiCulture Erasmus+ project include the Digital Skills and Social Inclusion for Creative Industries MOOC Courses available online and through blended learning, the Integrated Virtual Learning Hub including an innovative mobile app aimed at low-skilled and at-risk adults, the Digital Skills e-assessment tool and Open Badges for Digital Skills. Together they will provide important new opportunities for low-skilled adults to access knowledge, gain new digital skills and inter-cultural competences and improve their chances of finding employment or performing better in their current employment.

The project addresses a gap in creative industries (CI) education where there is low emphasis on the use of new digital technologies, entrepreneurship (project management) and both recent graduates and existing employees lack important skills.

The DigiCulture – Improving the Digital Competences and Social Inclusion of Adults in Creative Industries – project focus on openness and inclusive in education. It involves the use and development of an open online and mobile course Digital Skills and Social Inclusion for Creative Industries, built as a Massive Open Online Course (MOOC), an innovative adult educational program of 13 modules available in English, Romanian, German, Italian, Lithuanian, Danish and Gaelic, integrating new Open Education Resources (OER) and accessible to people with limited digital skills.

The diverse partnership reunites adult education centres from technical universities, art and humanities universities, SMEs with expertise in eLearning and in art, professionals in eLearning associations and associations for European Capital of Culture 2021 and 2022, involved as partners and associates.

The project targets young adults who are unemployed, staff and volunteers of European Capitals of Culture, creative industries adults with low digital skills, at levels of seniority, experience or level of craft, actors in traditional skills activities, museums, media, architecture, humanities. Many cultural actors are not attached to any formal institution, being freelancers, members of disadvantaged groups (unemployed, with mental health problems, disabilities or economically challenged) or from minority groups. Gaining digital skills will improve their career opportunities by providing access to new marketing tools, new distribution markets through Internet access and ecommerce, and adding the possibility of new forms of digital expression to their work.

The Objectives of DigiCulture are:

1. To enhance awareness of the need for training in digital skills for the creative industries.
2. To design and validate cross-country Guidelines for Digital Competences for Creative Industries.
3. To create an Integrated Virtual Learning Hub as an online and mobile.
4. To design, develop and deliver a Digital Skills and Social Inclusion for Creative Industries Course, OER translated into all partners' languages, delivered as a mix of blended learning course and, a fully online MOOC type course for the target group.
5. To improve the achievement and recognition of digital skills through formal and informal learning by introducing Digital Skills e-assessment and Open Badges for adult education in CI.
6. To provide engaging and effective learning experiences in the Digital Skills for CI course.

7. To enhance collaboration between education providers, universities, cultural and heritage institutions and associations, cultural actors, workers and volunteers.
8. To provide evidence about how achievement, assessment and validation of digital skills contributes to the uptake of new skills in creative industries.

The project will directly train 1,200 people online and through blended learning. At the end of DigiCulture all the tools and materials will be under the Creative Commons License, available online or on DSC mobile app available for all.

Main target groups of the project: The project aims to create a sustainable and efficient education program dedicated to adult learners with low digital skills and low-qualified adults involved in the creative industries sector.